Agile

Project Management

Lead Your Team to Success through these Principles and Practices

David A. Cohen

Table of Contents

Introduction

In dynamic business environment, one concept stands tall as a symbol of flexibility, teamwork, and customer-focus: Agile. This guide aims to decode the core of Agile, illustrating it not just as a set of procedures but as a belief system centered on creating value and welcoming alterations.

Agile's inception is deeply linked with software development, an area where rapid technological shifts necessitated a more versatile stance towards project management. Yet, as we'll uncover, Agile's tenets have seeped beyond software, resonating with areas like marketing, HR, and manufacturing. This accentuates an essential notion: Agile is not just a methodology; it's a perspective capable of reshaping our problem-solving strategies and solution delivery.

Starting with its bedrock concepts, we'll articulate what sets Agile apart from classical project management tactics. We'll navigate through diverse Agile strategies, spotlighting their specific features and utility. Beyond theoretical discussions, we'll bring in tangible narratives from varied fields to emphasize the tangible benefits of adopting Agile.

The main goal of this book is simple: to provide a comprehensive guide that sheds light on the what, why, and how of Agile, empowering you to harness its potential for transformative results.

Let's begin this way, seeking clarity, insight, and the tools to navigate the complex, yet rewarding world of Agile!

Chapter One: A Brief Look at Agile

In the early 90s, the tech world was largely governed by a conventional form of project management, frequently identified as the waterfall model. This process entailed subdividing tasks into consecutive stages, where each phase's outcomes dictated the next one. Regrettably, this model was marked with numerous drawbacks. The unyielding nature of the waterfall method failed to accommodate fluctuating requirements or unexpected hurdles, culminating in projects exceeding budget, straying from schedules, or in extreme scenarios, final products that became outdated upon their completion.

In such a vibrant setting, the demand for a more malleable, adaptive strategy became strikingly obvious. This led to the inception of the Agile approach, a response to the need for adaptability, assimilation of fresh data, and a commitment to offering incremental, ongoing value to clients.

Fast forward to 2001, when a team of seventeen innovative thinkers, known for their groundbreaking contributions to software development, assembled in Snowbird, Utah. Despite employing a variety of methodologies like Scrum, Extreme Programming (XP), and Dynamic Systems Development Method (DSDM), they were united by a shared discontentment with the predominant project management standards.

The result of their assembly was the Agile Manifesto, a succinct expression of core values and principles aimed at refining the software development process. The Agile Manifesto underscored the importance of people and interactions over systems and tools, functioning software over thorough documentation, client collaboration over contractual negotiations, and adaptability over adherence to a plan. This document served as the cornerstone of the present-day Agile methodology.

Following the Manifesto, Agile swiftly gained popularity owing to its potential for quicker delivery, superior product quality, and enhanced client satisfaction. Businesses began to appreciate the advantages of this cyclical approach that encouraged cooperation, embraced change, and delivered value bit by bit.

The Agile approach did more than just question the established project management practices in the software world, it reformed them. The defining characteristic of Agile, its inherent pliability and aptitude for adaptation, became its prime attraction as it addressed the innately unpredictable nature of software development.

Currently, Agile has surpassed the confines of software development and has been adopted by various sectors, including marketing, manufacturing, and even organization management. It has not only persisted but flourished amidst evolving landscapes, adapting and progressing as it was intended to.

The trajectory of Agile from its inception to its widespread application today signifies a shift from rigid, linear thinking to a dynamic, cyclical approach. As we delve further into the Agile domain in subsequent chapters, we aim to unpack how this method can be effectively implemented, clarify the roles and rituals in Agile, navigate potential obstacles, and ultimately, leverage the potential of Agile for organizational triumph.

Why Agile?

As the digital arena became more intricate and the pace of transformation quickened, companies were on the hunt for a method that could keep up. This is where Agile entered the picture, bringing a transformative change. Unlike conventional strategies, Agile methodologies provided enterprises the ability to rapidly adjust to changes, elevate product quality, and ensure customer satisfaction.

The primary mission of Agile is to foster adaptability and welcome modifications. It achieves this by deconstructing large-scale projects into manageable work segments, known as iterations or sprints. Each of these iterations is a small-scale project on its own, encompassing stages of planning, analyzing, designing, testing, and documenting. After each sprint, a functional product is delivered, making sure that value is continually handed to the client.

This incremental and repetitive technique allows Agile teams to effectively adapt to changes. If a project's prerequisites shift - as they frequently do - teams have the flexibility to adjust, modifying future sprints to include the changes without upending the whole project. Agile's adaptability is arguably its key strength, empowering organizations to create products that genuinely cater to their customers' needs and aspirations.

Agile has made a significant imprint on the domain of project management and beyond. It has allowed organizations to launch products quicker, enhance team productivity, and heighten customer satisfaction. According to the 2017 Pulse of the Profession report by the Project Management Institute (PMI), Agile projects have a 28% higher success rate compared to traditional projects.

Moreover, Agile's emphasis on collaboration, communication, and empowering teams has had a profound influence on organizational cultures. Agile environments cultivate a growth-oriented mindset, promote constant learning, and value every team member's contributions. Teams become more unified and efficient, resulting in improved problem-solving and innovation.

Agile has also shaped customer relations. The direct participation of customers or their proxies (product owners) in the development process guarantees that the end product meets customer expectations. This collaborative strategy enhances customer satisfaction and heightens the chances of project success.

One frequently discussed aspect in project management pertains to the comparison between Agile and conventional methodologies. Though each approach has its unique merits and can be advantageous depending on the nature and context of a project, they significantly diverge in their ideologies, practices, and overall attitude.

Conventional project management, epitomized by techniques such as the Waterfall model, follows a linear and sequential pattern. The lifespan of a project commences with thorough planning, succeeded by a sequence of design, execution, testing, deployment, and upkeep stages. Every phase hinges on the culmination of the preceding one, with scarce opportunity for revisions or iteration once a phase is finished.

This strategy possesses its advantages, particularly for projects where prerequisites are well-established and unlikely to fluctuate, and the result can be reliably foreseen from the beginning. Nonetheless, this inflexibility can be a shortcoming in more dynamic settings, where requirements might evolve or new data could emerge, influencing the project.

Conversely, Agile project management is accepting of change and uncertainty. Agile projects are compartmentalized into small, manageable chunks, or iterations. Every iteration encompasses all phases of the project life cycle—planning, designing, building, testing—and culminates in a usable product. This implies that even if the project is interrupted or its course alters, value has been delivered already.

Furthermore, Agile underscores continuous collaboration among team members and stakeholders, regular introspection and adjustment, and a focus on providing working software over comprehensive documentation. This approach cultivates adaptability, swift responses to change, and incessant enhancement.

Agile Principles and Values

As we already know, at the heart of Agile project management are its fundamental principles and ideals, eloquently outlined in the Agile Manifesto. This Manifesto, penned in 2001, serves as the bedrock on which all Agile methodologies stand and flourish. To genuinely fathom the core of Agile, grasping these principles and values is crucial.

Agile Values

The Agile Manifesto begins with four primary values:

Individuals and Interactions over Processes and Tools: The Agile Manifesto, the essential document for Agile methodologies, underscores the significance of people and communication over procedures and tools. Although procedures and tools are integral to any project, Agile contends that they shouldn't be the primary driving force. The spotlight should instead be on the people involved and their interactions. Agile promotes regular conversation, close teamwork, and mutual understanding among all team members. By capitalizing on the talents, innovation, and knowledge of each individual and cultivating a culture of collaboration and unity, Agile can generate efficient, adaptable teams capable of producing high-quality results. Agile acknowledges that every team member possesses a unique set of abilities and viewpoints, and the most potent solutions often arise from harnessing these diverse talents in a transparent, cooperative setting.

Working Software over Comprehensive Documentation: Conventional methodologies frequently demand extensive documentation before, during, and after development. This may encompass detailed strategies, designs, and specifications, among others. While documentation is essential for system comprehension and future maintenance, Agile methodologies argue that it should not take precedence over a functioning product. Agile concentrates on delivering a working product that brings value to the customer as swiftly as possible. The concept is that a working product is the prime indicator of progress, and it's more beneficial to devote time to developing features that deliver immediate value to the customer rather than generating exhaustive documentation. That's not to suggest that documentation is overlooked in Agile; it's just simplified to the most necessary components to ensure clarity and maintainability.

Customer Collaboration over Contract Negotiation: Agile methodologies consider client engagement as critical to any project's success. Instead of merely negotiating a contract at the project's onset and delivering a product at the end, Agile teams pursue continual client engagement throughout the project. Regular feedback sessions, demonstrations of work in progress, and active participation of customers in setting priorities ensure that the final product closely matches the customer's current and evolving needs. This continual collaboration allows Agile teams to better comprehend customer needs and expectations, and adjust the product accordingly, leading to higher customer satisfaction and a more successful product.

Responding to Change over Following a Plan: Traditional project management methods often emphasize initial planning, with a detailed plan established at the beginning of a project and any deviations from this plan seen as issues. Conversely, Agile methodologies accept that change is an inherent aspect of any project, especially in intricate, rapidly evolving environments. Agile encourages teams to maintain flexibility and be responsive to change, whether it be changes in the market, technology, customer requirements, or other factors. Rather than strictly sticking to a predetermined plan, Agile teams employ iterative development and feedback loops to continually reevaluate and adjust their plans as needed. This adaptability enables Agile teams to better tackle unforeseen challenges and seize new opportunities, leading to more successful outcomes.

Agile Principles

The Agile Manifesto is further underpinned by twelve principles, which serve as a guiding light for implementing Agile practices:

Customer Satisfaction: At the apex of Agile methodologies' priorities is client satisfaction. The primary determinant of success in an Agile project isn't the tally of features integrated or rigid fidelity to initial blueprints, but instead, it's the delivery of valuable software that caters to the client's needs and anticipations. To guarantee this, Agile teams actively involve clients in the developmental process, constantly inviting feedback and making modifications based on this feedback. This client-centric approach not only aids in fabricating software that closely mirrors what the client desires but also nurtures a relationship of trust and cooperation, which can lead to heightened levels of client satisfaction and enduring engagement.

Welcoming Change: A pivotal principle of Agile methodologies is accommodating evolving requirements, even late in the development. Conventional project management methodologies frequently perceive alterations, especially last-minute changes, as a problem due to the disturbance they pose to the original blueprint. Conversely, Agile approaches view change as an opportunity to enhance the product and create something that better fulfills the client's needs. This adaptability originates from the understanding that the client's needs, market dynamics, and technological landscapes can evolve over time. Therefore, Agile approaches exploit change for the client's competitive benefit, ensuring that the final product remains pertinent, valuable, and high-quality even in a dynamic environment.

Frequent Delivery: Agile methodologies underscore the regular delivery of functioning software. Instead of waiting until the project's end to deliver a final product, Agile teams strive to deliver functional increments of the product regularly, ranging from a few weeks to a few months, with a preference for the shorter timescale. This approach, often labeled "incremental" or "iterative" development, yields several benefits. It allows clients to start reaping the product's benefits earlier, gives them regular opportunities to offer feedback, and enables the team to test and refine the product continually. The regular delivery of functioning software also helps sustain momentum and morale within the Agile team, as they can observe tangible progress and receive immediate feedback on their work.

Cooperative Effort: Agile methodologies place a significant emphasis on cooperation, particularly between business individuals (such as product owners, stakeholders, or clients) and developers. Instead of interacting only at the project's inception and conclusion, as is often the case in traditional methodologies, Agile posits that business individuals and developers should collaborate daily throughout the project. This ongoing collaboration nurtures a shared understanding of the project goals, enhances decision-making by incorporating diverse viewpoints, and ensures that the developmental work remains tightly aligned with business objectives and client needs. The collaborative environment also encourages mutual respect, understanding, and shared responsibility among team members, contributing to a more effective and satisfying work process.

Support and Trust: Agile methodologies underline the significance of developing projects around inspired individuals. They postulate that the secret to a triumphant project does not merely reside in the accurate technologies or meticulous plans, but in procuring the right individuals, and then enabling them to excel. In Agile, teams are provided with the environment and support crucial to accomplishing their duties, which might encompass suitable tools, a facilitative work setting, clear communication pathways, and access to necessary data or resources. Beyond this, Agile underscores the importance of trusting these individuals to accomplish the task at hand. This trust inculcates a sense of responsibility, incites team members to take the initiative, encourages innovation, and cultivates a culture of responsibility and accountability.

IFace-to-Face Communication: While written documents, emails, and other modes of communication hold their importance, Agile methodologies argue that in-person discussion is the most effective and efficient method of transmitting information to and within a development team. This immediate interaction cultivates clear and instant comprehension, enables prompt feedback, and minimizes the possibility of miscommunication or misunderstanding. Face-to-face communication also fosters stronger relationships and a more harmonious team, as it permits team members to engage more intimately with each other and comprehend each other's viewpoints and notions. In circumstances where physical in-person communication is unattainable, such as remote or distributed teams, video conferencing or other forms of live, interactive communication can serve as effective substitutes.

Working Software: Agile methodologies prioritize operational software as the paramount indicator of progress. Instead of focusing on the completion of individual duties or phases, or the production of extensive documentation, Agile posits that the most meaningful sign of progress is the delivery of functional software that provides value to the client. This emphasis encourages teams to concentrate on the essential features and functions that directly add to the software's value, and diminishes the time spent on non-essential activities. By delivering operational software regularly, Agile teams can also accumulate frequent feedback, identify and address problems early, and perpetually enhance the software's quality and relevance.

Sustainable Development: Agile processes advocate for enduring development. This signifies that the pace of work should be sustainable, enabling the sponsors, developers, and users to uphold a steady, predictable pace indefinitely. The concept is to evade practices that may lead to burnout or significant fluctuations in productivity, such as excessive overtime, high-pressure deadlines, or unrealistic expectations. Sustainable development can result in higher-quality outcomes, as it allows for regular periods of reflection and improvement, prevents hasty or negligent work, and maintains the team's motivation and productivity over the long term. To support this, Agile practices often include regular breaks, flexible schedules, a balanced workload, and a focus on the long-term health and well-being of the team members.

Technical Excellence: Agile methodologies stress the significance of continuous focus on technical prowess and quality design. This involves maintaining excellent code quality standards, utilizing optimal practices in software development, routinely refining the code to enhance its structure and readability, and investing in quality design principles. Agile comprehends that technical debt, such as untidy code, quick fixes, or inferior design decisions, can decelerate development and decrease agility over time. Therefore, it advocates for spending the necessary time to perform tasks correctly from the beginning. This attention to technical proficiency and quality design not only improves the software's quality but also renders it more maintainable, scalable, and adaptable to changes, thereby enhancing the team's agility and productivity.

Simplicity: Another critical principle in Agile methodologies is simplicity, often defined as "the art of maximizing the amount of work not done." This involves concentrating on what's truly needed and avoiding superfluous or redundant tasks. In software development, this could mean giving priority to essential features, utilizing uncomplicated and direct solutions, and avoiding over-engineering or speculative development (i.e., developing features or functionalities that aren't presently required but might be useful in the future). By focusing on value-adding elements and eliminating unnecessary complexity, teams can deliver products more quickly and efficiently, making adaptation to changes easier and reducing the risk of introducing errors or complications.

Self-Organizing Teams: Agile methodologies champion the concept of self-organizing teams. This implies that instead of a top-down management approach, Agile teams are given the freedom to organize their work, make decisions, and solve problems. This approach relies on the belief that the individuals who are most familiar with the work are best suited to make decisions about its execution. It encourages ownership, empowerment, creativity, and collaboration within the team. It also encourages team members to assume various roles and responsibilities as required, contributing to the team's flexibility and versatility. Agile suggests that the finest architectures, requirements, and designs often emerge from these self-organizing teams, as they possess a deep understanding of the project, the flexibility to adapt to changes, and a vested interest in the quality of their work.

Regular Reflection and Adjustment: Agile methodologies encourage teams to engage in regular reflection and adjustment. This usually takes the form of regular meetings or retrospectives, where the team reviews their work, discusses the positives and negatives, and decides on actions to enhance their effectiveness. This reflection allows the team to identify and tackle issues, learn from their experiences, and continuously improve their skills, practices, and processes. After reflecting, the team then modifies its behavior, strategies, or plans as needed. This cycle of reflection and adjustment helps the team adapt to changes, enhance their performance, and become more efficient and effective over time. It also cultivates a culture of continuous learning and improvement within the team.

These tenets and guidelines serve as the foundation of Agile project management. They advocate for a mentality that appreciates teamwork, customer gratification, high-quality functional software, and the agility to adjust to change.

Agile Methodologies: Scrum, Kanban, XP, Lean

While the Agile Manifesto provides the core principles and values, various Agile methodologies offer specific practices and structures to embody these principles. In this chapter, we'll explore some of the most common Agile methodologies: Scrum, Kanban, Extreme Programming (XP), and Lean Software Development.

Scrum

As one of the most commonly employed Agile methodologies, Scrum relies on the concept of iterative and progressive development. Each cycle, or sprint, usually spans one to four weeks and targets to deliver a potentially launch-ready product increment. Here are the specifics:

Roles: Scrum outlines three fundamental roles. The Product Owner oversees the product backlog, which encompasses all tasks or features required for the product. The Product Owner also ranks these tasks based on their business value. The Scrum Master, on the other hand, enables the Scrum process, works to eliminate obstacles that the team may encounter, and ensures adherence to Scrum principles. Finally, the Development Team is tasked with implementing the work defined in the sprint.

Ceremonies: Crucial Scrum ceremonies incorporate the Sprint Planning meeting, where the team defines the scope of the upcoming sprint; the Daily Scrum, a short daily meeting to coordinate the team's tasks and plan for the forthcoming day's work; the Sprint Review, where the team examines the work concluded in the sprint and discusses the product backlog for the next sprint; and the Sprint Retrospective, a reflection meeting where the team pinpoints areas for enhancement.

Artifacts: Scrum also employs several artifacts to track progress and manage tasks. These include the Product Backlog, encompassing a list of all desired work for the product; the Sprint Backlog, a subset of the product backlog that the team commits to finalizing in the current sprint; and the Increment, the aggregate of all the product backlog items accomplished during a sprint.

Kanban

Kanban is an Agile methodology that emphasizes visual task management and limiting the amount of work in progress. It originates from the manufacturing industry but has been effectively adapted for software development.

Visualization: Kanban uses a board (physical or digital) to illustrate the workflow. The board features columns representing distinct stages of the workflow, and cards denoting individual work items are relocated across the board as they advance through these stages. This visualization makes it easy to observe the work status, identify bottlenecks, and monitor progress.

Limiting WIP: One of the core principles of Kanban is constraining work in progress (WIP). This means that the number of work items in any given stage of the workflow is restricted to a pre-determined limit. Limiting WIP assists in avoiding overload, maintaining a stable flow of work, and rapidly highlighting bottlenecks or blockages.

Continuous Flow: Unlike Scrum, which operates in time-boxed iterations, Kanban runs on the principle of continuous flow. Work items are introduced into the system as the team has the capacity to manage them, rather than being pushed into the workflow based on time. This method promotes flexibility, as it enables the team to adapt to alterations or new priorities swiftly.

Roles and Ceremonies: Unlike Scrum, Kanban does not mandate specific roles or ceremonies. However, analogous to Scrum, Kanban encourages collaboration, transparency, and continuous improvement.

Extreme Programming (XP)

Extreme Programming stands as an Agile methodology, aiming to enhance software quality while maintaining the flexibility to cater to fluctuating customer requirements.

Practices: Several techniques define XP, including pair programming (two coders collaborating on a single task), continuous integration (frequent integration of changes into the main codebase to spot and resolve integration problems early), test-driven development (formulating tests before coding, which dictates the software's design), and refactoring (reorganizing existing code without modifying its outward behavior, thereby improving its legibility and decreasing complexity).

High customer engagement and swift feedback loops: Extreme Programming advocates for ongoing dialogue with the customer, incorporating them as an essential team member for defining and prioritizing features. This active involvement guarantees the software developed matches their needs and expectations. Swift feedback loops also play a significant role in XP, with regular releases enabling the team to obtain rapid feedback and adapt the product accordingly.

Values: Five fundamental values underpin XP - simplicity (build only what's necessary), communication (transparent, clear, and direct interaction among team members and customers), feedback (via tests, new releases, and customer input), courage (to tackle changes and address issues directly), and respect (among team members depending on each other for the project's success).

Technical Practices: XP's technical practices are crafted to handle changing requirements without triggering excessive rework, while continually delivering high-quality software. These practices promote continuous design enhancement and involve frequent assessment of the code's fitness for its purpose.

Lean Software Development

Lean Software Development, drawing from its predecessor, Lean Manufacturing, centers around maximizing customer value and minimizing waste.

Principles: Lean Software Development principles consist of eliminating waste (eradicating anything that doesn't contribute value to the customer), amplifying learning (welcoming change and constantly improving), delaying decision-making (preserving options for as long as feasible), delivering as quickly as possible (the quicker the delivery, the faster the feedback), empowering the team (providing autonomy and cultivating a sense of ownership), building integrity (designing a consistent and cohesive system), and viewing the whole (understanding the larger context beyond individual elements).

Practices: Lean practices aim to optimize efficiency by reducing waste, which could arise in many forms, such as unnecessary code or functionality, delay in the software development process, vague or quickly changing requirements, etc. The goal is to establish a lean process that produces precisely what the customer needs, no more or less.

Continuous Improvement: The Lean approach endorses a culture of continuous improvement, reflecting the philosophy of Kaizen from Lean Manufacturing. Kaizen focuses on small, daily improvements that result in significant long-term enhancement. The aim is to nurture a work culture where all employees actively contribute to improving the company. This philosophy helps instill a sense of purpose in the team and nurtures a culture where everyone is committed to betterment.

While each of these Agile methodologies brings its unique viewpoints and practices, they all align with the fundamental Agile values and principles. They can be blended or tailored as needed, enabling organizations to adopt the strategy that best suits their context and requirements. Although they vary in specifics, they all strive to deliver value swiftly and regularly, collaborate closely with the customer, and respond effectively to change.

Chapter Two: Implementing Agile

The formation of an Agile team is a pivotal initial move in starting your Agile way. Such teams form the essence of Agile methodologies as they are the entities that create value and deliver the product. An Agile team isn't just a collection of individuals working together; it is an integrated unit that self-organizes, collaborates intensively, and constantly adjusts to yield the best results.

Below are the principal steps and factors to consider when forming an Agile team:

Form a Cross-Functional Team

The initial step in applying an Agile project is to form a cross-functional team. This means recruiting professionals with a variety of skills needed to execute the project.

Incorporation of Roles: A cross-functional team includes a range of roles necessary to the development process like business analysts, UX/UI designers, software developers, quality assurance testers, etc. This ensures that the team possesses all the necessary skills to convert an idea into a functioning product.

Collaboration and Efficiency: A crucial benefit of a cross-functional team is that it encourages collaboration and facilitates quick decision-making as everyone necessary for making a decision is already part of the team. This structure minimizes the need for transitions between separate teams, which could lead to delays and miscommunications.

Learning Opportunities: Another advantage of a cross-functional team is that it offers learning chances for all team members. They gain insights into different perspectives, methods, and expertise, enhancing their professional development and overall team performance.

Clarify Roles

While Agile supports self-organization and collaboration, it is equally important to define roles and responsibilities clearly.

Agile Roles: Depending on the Agile methodology applied, different roles are present. For instance, in Scrum, the three main roles are the Product Owner (tasked with maximizing the product's value and managing the product backlog), the Scrum Master (facilitates the Scrum process and helps everyone comprehend Scrum practices and values), and the Development Team (carries out the work).

Clarity and Purpose: Clearly outlined roles provide team members with a sense of purpose and responsibility. Everyone should understand their individual contribution towards achieving the project goals, leading to a more efficient and effective team.

Emphasize Collaboration and Communication

Agile methodologies are based on principles of collaboration and open communication.

Agile Workspace: Whether in a physical or virtual environment, the workspace should foster interaction among team members. The setup should facilitate easy and quick exchanges of ideas and information.

Agile Practices: Practices like daily stand-ups, which offer a platform for updating the team on what was achieved the previous day and what is planned for the current day, and regular retrospectives, where the team reflects on the past sprint and identifies areas for improvement, cultivate a culture of communication and collaboration.

Create a Backlog

The product backlog is a crucial tool for an Agile team, encompassing all the work that needs to be done on the project.

Nature of Backlog: The backlog is an ordered list of features, bug fixes, technical work, and knowledge acquisition required for effective product development. The items are usually written in the form of user stories.

Backlog Management: The Product Owner typically handles the creation, prioritization, and updating of the backlog. The items should be continuously refined and reprioritized based on customer feedback, market fluctuations, and team capacity. The backlog provides direction and keeps the team focused on delivering value to the customer.

Set Up Agile Practices and Tools

Implementing Agile methodologies and utilizing appropriate tools are essential elements of Agile project management.

Agile Techniques: Depending on the selected Agile strategy, various techniques can be utilized by the team. For example, Scrum teams function within time-limited cycles known as sprints, Extreme Programming (XP) promotes pair programming, and almost all Agile groups hold daily stand-up meetings to discuss advancements and obstacles. These methodologies help the team maintain focus, boost quality, and enhance communication.

Agile Soft: There is an array of digital resources available to support Agile methodologies, such as JIRA, Trello, and Asana. These resources often include options for creating and managing a product backlog, scheduling and tracking sprints, visualizing ongoing work (such as a Kanban board), and managing project documentation. The resource choice depends on the team's specific requirements and the project's nature.

Foster a Culture of Trust and Respect

Trust and esteem are fundamental to any Agile team's culture.

Psychological Safety: Team members should feel secure expressing their thoughts and ideas, raising concerns, and taking measured risks without fear of judgment or reprisal. They should be able to depend on each other, respecting the unique abilities, experiences, and perspectives that each member contributes to the team.

Accountability: In an atmosphere of trust and esteem, team members are more inclined to make and fulfill commitments, and to hold each other accountable. This cultivates a sense of shared responsibility and ownership of the team's tasks.

Leadership Role: Constructing such a culture requires effort from everyone in the team, particularly from the leaders. Leaders should exemplify the behavior they want to see, fostering an environment that promotes open communication, mutual esteem, and trust.

Commit to Continuous Improvement

An identifying characteristic of Agile teams is their dedication to continually enhancing their processes, products, skills, and relationships.

Frequent Retrospectives: Agile strategies typically incorporate the practice of frequent retrospectives—specific meetings at the end of each cycle to reflect on what went well, what didn't, and what can be enhanced. This allows teams to learn from their experiences and make necessary alterations.

Culture of Learning and Adaptation: Continuous improvement should be embedded in the team's culture. It's not just about enhancing processes, but also about personal growth and developing more effective methods to work together as a team. This requires a mindset of learning, adaptation, and innovation.

Experimentation: Continuous improvement often involves trying out new ideas and approaches, evaluating the outcomes, and then adjusting based on what was learned. This reinforces the Agile principle of being receptive to change.

Communication and Collaboration Tools

In Agile environments, having effective and efficient communication is essential as it involves swift adaptation to changes, collaboration within team members, and frequent client engagement.

Instant Communication: Platforms such as Slack and Microsoft Teams offer instant, informal communication and speedy decision-making, mirroring the pace and convenience of face-to-face conversations in virtual settings. They also support the creation of different channels for diverse topics, projects, or groups.

Document Collaboration and Sharing: Services like Google Workspace and Microsoft 365 permit team members to generate, share, and collaboratively revise documents in real time, ensuring everyone is updated and mitigating the risk of outdated versions or misinterpretations.

Video Meetings: Platforms like Zoom and Microsoft Teams also offer video meeting capabilities. This is particularly important for distributed Agile teams, as it allows direct communication, virtual stand-ups, sprint planning, and retrospectives.

Continuous Integration/Continuous Delivery (CI/CD)

Applications CI/CD methodologies are integral to Agile and DevOps, supporting regular and dependable software releases.

Continuous Integration: This practice involves programmers consistently merging their code alterations into a central repository, where automated builds and tests are performed. Applications like Jenkins, CircleCI, or Travis CI assist in automating this process, swiftly identifying integration issues and reducing the time and effort required for manual integration.

Continuous Delivery: This extends CI by automatically deploying all code changes to a testing or production environment. Applications like Jenkins, GitLab CI/CD, and Spinnaker can automate this process, accelerating delivery and minimizing the risks and effort associated with manual deployments.

Testing and Quality Assurance Applications

In Agile development, testing is interwoven throughout the lifecycle, rather than being a distinct phase.

Automated Testing: Applications like Selenium, JUnit, and TestNG enable automated testing, which can significantly increase test coverage and frequency while reducing the time and effort required for manual testing.

Behavior-Driven Development (BDD) and Test-Driven Development (TDD): These practices involve crafting tests before the code is developed. Applications like Cucumber and SpecFlow can support BDD by enabling tests to be written in a more natural language style.

Training and Support

To ensure successful adoption of these tools, teams need appropriate training and support.

Education: This could include formal training sessions, online tutorials, or hands-on coaching. The focus should be on how to utilize the tools in the context of the team's Agile practices, rather than just technical training.

Support: It's crucial to select tools that offer robust support in terms of documentation, customer service, and an active user community. This will help resolve any issues quickly and enable the team to fully leverage the tools' capabilities.

Planning and Prioritizing of Work

The groundwork of a successful Agile project lies in the initial planning and prioritization of tasks. It's about getting the team on the same page about what needs to be created and in what order, based on the value it imparts to the customer and the business. Let's explore how to effectively carry out this crucial stage.

Identify and Understand Stakeholders: Recognizing stakeholders involves pinpointing those who are directly or indirectly influenced by your product or service, or those who can affect the successful delivery of the product.

Internal stakeholders could encompass team members, other employees, and executives, while external stakeholders could span from customers, suppliers, investors, to regulatory authorities. Once stakeholders are recognized, understanding their needs and expectations becomes paramount. This comprehension is not just about knowing what stakeholders desire, but also how they derive value from your product. User interviews can yield detailed insights into stakeholder needs, enabling you to capture the subtleties of their requirements. Surveys can produce numerical data about stakeholder preferences and can be utilized to reach a larger audience. Workshops, on the other hand, are outstanding platforms for cooperation and brainstorming, where various stakeholders can express their viewpoints and contribute to the product vision.

Prioritize the Backlog: Arranging the backlog is the process of ordering the tasks or 'stories' in your backlog based on their significance or urgency. A balanced collaboration between the product owner, the team, and other crucial stakeholders is vital in this process to ensure a comprehensive understanding of what needs to be accomplished. The MoSCoW method categorizes tasks into Must have, Should have, Could have, and Won't have, offering a simple yet effective way of determining priority. Other methods such as the value/risk matrix evaluate tasks based on their potential value against the associated risks. ROI scoring assigns a score based on the anticipated return on investment of each task. The RICE scoring model prioritizes tasks based on Reach, Impact, Confidence, and Effort, offering a balanced view of priority considering both the potential benefits and the associated effort and confidence.

Estimate Effort: Quantifying effort involves determining the amount of work and time required to complete each story in the backlog. Agile teams typically use methods such as Planning Poker for estimation. In this approach, each team member offers their estimate for each task, followed by a discussion for vastly differing estimates, leading to a consensus. This process not only leverages expert opinions but also fosters a shared understanding of the tasks among the team members. The estimation allows the team to plan better, ensures an equal workload, and aids in prioritizing tasks.

Plan the First Iteration: With a prioritized backlog and effort estimates ready, the team is prepared to plan the first iteration, or 'sprint' in Scrum parlance. This involves selecting a set of high-priority tasks from the backlog that the team commits to completing in the sprint. Caution should be exercised to avoid overcommitting - the chosen tasks should align with the team's capacity. Overcommitting can lead to stress, hurried work, and compromised quality. This planning process encourages focus and enhances the team's morale by delivering completed work at the end of each iteration.

After the initial planning and prioritization, the team needs to keep track of the backlog, conduct regular inspections, and be ready to reprioritize tasks if necessary. This is not a sign of poor planning but a response to the inherent uncertainties and changes in the environment. Feedback from stakeholders, lessons from completed tasks, or shifts in market conditions can all prompt adjustments. An Agile team embraces these changes to ensure that their work continues to provide the highest value.

Chapter Three: Roles and Responsibilities

A highly effective Agile team is distinguished by distinct roles, each bringing specific responsibilities and contributions to the Agile process. Let's examine the principal roles in a typical Agile setup, specifically within the Scrum framework: the Product Owner, the Scrum Master, and the Team Member.

Product Owner

The Product Owner (PO) acts as the customer's representative within the Agile team. They are charged with ensuring the team provides the greatest value to the business.

The Product Owner (PO) is the chief keeper of the product backlog, a storage area of all possible work items—from new features, enhancements, technical improvements, to bug repairs—for a product. In administering the backlog, the PO's initial duty is to produce well-defined, valuable, and viable work items, often known as 'user stories'. These stories should be articulated concisely, emphasizing the result for the user or business, rather than dictating how the work should be accomplished. The PO also regularly refines and maintains the backlog, ensuring that the details of the stories are updated and are ready to be undertaken by the team. Prioritizing the backlog is a crucial aspect of the PO's role. The PO employs various prioritization techniques and cooperates with stakeholders to rank the stories based on factors like customer and business value, risk, and effort. The goal is to ensure that the team always embarks on the most valuable and crucial items first.

As a main point of contact for the product, the PO frequently communicates with numerous stakeholders—internal teams, customers, executives, suppliers, and regulatory bodies. The PO actively strives to comprehend the varied needs, expectations, and limitations of these stakeholders. This involves not just listening but also probing the right questions to discover hidden needs. Stakeholder feedback is a wealth of information that the PO uses to refine the product vision, backlog, and priorities. In addition to gathering inputs, the PO also aligns stakeholder expectations about what the team can deliver and when. The PO conveys the product roadmap, progress, and challenges, promoting transparency and trust. Consistent and proactive communication aids in managing potential disputes and ensures that everyone is working towards the same objectives.

As development advances, the PO plays a strategic role in decision-making. The PO is not typically engaged in how the team does the work, but they are accountable for deciding what functionality and features are incorporated in the product. This involves assessing the trade-offs between different options and making decisions that maximize value. For instance, when confronted with scope creep or schedule overruns, the PO may need to decide whether to postpone less critical features to future iterations. The PO also resolves uncertainties, answers queries, and provides feedback to the team during the development phases. Their goal is to ensure that the team's effort aligns with the product vision and delivers the anticipated value to customers and the business. The PO stays in tune with changes in the market, user feedback, and business strategy, and integrates these insights into the development process, steering the product in the right direction.

Scrum Master

The Scrum Master acts as the guide and mentor for the Agile team, aiding the team in understanding and properly applying Scrum and other Agile methodologies.

As a Scrum expert, the Scrum Master holds a critical role in advocating Agile methods within the team. They make certain that each team member is thoroughly familiar with the principles, values, and practices tied to Scrum, such as empiricism, self-management, and iterative progress. This involves organizing training sessions, supplying resources for self-learning, and addressing any questions team members may have. The Scrum Master also cultivates an Agile mentality, promoting qualities like adaptability, collaboration, customer-focus, and continuous learning. They ensure that Scrum practices are not simply perceived as procedures to follow, but as tools that assist the team in delivering value quicker and more efficiently. Furthermore, the Scrum Master protects the team from external distractions, ensuring the team's concentration and compliance with Scrum processes.

Scrum ceremonies or events—Daily Scrum (or stand-ups), Sprint Planning, Sprint Review, and Sprint Retrospective—

are central to the Scrum framework, and the Scrum Master is the chief facilitator for these. During Daily Scrum, they make sure that the meetings are kept within the time limit and that discussions are centered on progress and roadblocks. In Sprint Planning, they ascertain that the team understands the scope of the sprint and that they collectively decide on the sprint goal and the set of backlog items to be worked on. In Sprint Review, the Scrum Master oversees the demonstration of the increment to stakeholders and collects their feedback. Finally, during the Sprint Retrospective, they encourage the team to reflect on the past sprint, pinpoint areas of improvement, and plan actions for the next sprint.

A significant responsibility of the Scrum Master is to recognize and eliminate hurdles, or 'blockers', that obstruct the team's progress. These obstacles can take various forms, from technical issues, like code conflicts or system downtime, to process issues, such as delays in decision making or lack of clarity in requirements. Sometimes, they may be interpersonal issues or conflicts within the team. The Scrum Master needs to be proactive, responsive, and resourceful in handling these issues. They may collaborate with the team to find solutions, escalate issues to management, or coordinate with other teams or departments to resolve dependencies. The goal is to clear the team's path, enabling them to concentrate on their work and achieve their sprint goals.

The Scrum Master fosters a culture of continual improvement, a fundamental principle of Agile and Scrum. They champion the retrospective practice, where the team regularly reflects on their performance and identifies opportunities to improve their processes, tools, skills, and interactions. The Scrum Master ensures that these retrospectives result in tangible improvement actions and that these actions are executed and their effects reviewed in subsequent sprints. They also assist the team in learning and applying new techniques and practices that increase their effectiveness. By advocating a safe and open environment, they encourage the team to experiment, learn from failures, and continuously enhance their performance and the value they deliver.

Team Member

The Development Team is responsible for delivering the product. They are self-organizing and cross-functional, which means they decide how to do the work and have all the skills necessary to deliver a potentially shippable product increment.

In the Scrum framework, the Development Team shoulders the responsibility of product delivery. This group is self-directed and cross-functional, signifying that they make choices on the method of work execution and are equipped with all requisite skills to furnish a potentially deliverable product increment.

Within an Agile backdrop, team members are engaged with user stories or tasks that are itemized in the sprint backlog. These tasks typically encompass diverse activities such as designing, coding, testing, and integrating, all aimed at yielding a functioning software component, referred to as an increment, by the end of each sprint cycle. The tasks are self-appointed, fostering a sense of personal responsibility and accountability among team members. Agile supports the concept of cross-functional teams, where members are skilled in various areas and can undertake diverse types of tasks. This range of skills aids in equitably distributing the workload and alleviating bottlenecks. Team members also abide by methodologies like Test-Driven Development (TDD) and Continuous Integration (CI) to maintain quality and mitigate integration risks. The purpose extends beyond mere task completion, striving to deliver value to the customer through a potentially shippable product increment.

Team members in an Agile setup are anticipated to collaborate closely. They exchange information, deliberate on issues, and collectively address problems. Practices such as pair programming are employed, where two developers collaborate on the same code—with one writing the code and the other reviewing it. Pair programming not only bolsters code quality by detecting errors at an early stage but also fosters knowledge exchange and learning. Similarly, methodologies like collective code ownership are practiced, where every team member is permitted and expected to modify any segment of the code, nurturing a sense of collective responsibility and reducing individual dependencies. Regular communication and collaboration contribute to a high-trust environment where team members can depend on one another, thereby enhancing team performance.

Agile teams are dedicated to ameliorating their practices, performance, and the value they deliver. A crucial method for this is the retrospective meeting conducted at the close of each sprint. In these meetings, team members reflect on their experiences, discussing successes and failures, and pinpointing areas of improvement. They brainstorm potential solutions and pledge to enact specific actions in the succeeding sprint. Continuous improvement isn't solely about processes and techniques—it also involves enhancing skills, collaboration, and team morale. Agile teams value learning and innovation. They are receptive to experimenting with new ideas and aren't intimidated by mistakes, viewing them instead as opportunities for learning and enhancement.

More about Role of Stakeholders

Stakeholders play a critical role in establishing the direction for any product or project. They contribute to the creation of the vision, articulating a clear, inspiring picture of the end goal. This vision acts as a compass, guiding all activities and decisions related to the project. Further, stakeholders set specific, measurable, achievable, relevant, and time-bound (SMART) goals, and key performance indicators (KPIs). These provide clarity about what success looks like and offer a roadmap for the Agile team. By aligning the project's purpose with its business value, stakeholders help the team grasp the significance of their work, driving motivation and commitment.

Also stakeholders are the source of the product's requirements. They express their needs and expectations as user stories, specifying who needs what and why. These stories become the foundation of the product backlog.

Stakeholders work closely with the Product Owner to prioritize the backlog, ranking items based on value, risk, and dependencies. By defining and prioritizing requirements, stakeholders ensure that the Agile team focuses its efforts on delivering the maximum value to the users and the business.

Agile is about iterative development and frequent feedback. Stakeholders are often involved in the sprint review meetings, where they assess the product increment developed during the sprint. They provide feedback on the delivered features and suggest adjustments, based on their evolving understanding of the market, users, and business environment. This constant engagement and feedback loop helps steer the product in the right direction and ensures that the final product meets stakeholder needs and expectations.

Stakeholders play a supportive role for the Agile team. They can assist in eliminating impediments that are beyond the team's control, providing necessary resources, and fostering a conducive environment for the team to work efficiently. They advocate for the team and the Agile approach within the organization, helping remove organizational barriers and fostering an Agile culture. Their support can boost the team's morale, productivity, and adherence to Agile principles.

Stakeholders are an integral part of team. They learn from each iteration, taking into account the feedback from users, performance metrics, and the team's experiences. They use these insights to refine their understanding, make better decisions, and enhance their collaboration with the Agile team. This ongoing learning helps them become better at handling uncertainty, managing change, and leading Agile projects.

Interactions Among Team Members

Agile emphasizes the shared accountability of the team for the success of the product. This ideology creates a cooperative environment where team members collaborate to complete tasks, rather than working in isolation. Cooperation allows for the merging of different skills, viewpoints, and experiences, resulting in more efficient problem-solving and decision-making. Agile practices like pair programming, where two developers work on the same code, and code audits, where code produced by one developer is inspected by others, embody this cooperative strategy. These practices not only improve the quality of work, but also encourage knowledge exchange and collective learning. Cooperation in Agile extends beyond the team, involving interactions with stakeholders, users, and other teams, strengthening the concept of common ownership and joint success.

Confidence and esteem constitute the foundation of an effective Agile team. Trust is established when team members consistently fulfill their commitments, demonstrate skills, and act with honesty. This breeds a secure environment where team members feel at ease sharing ideas, offering and accepting feedback, and acknowledging mistakes. Esteem, conversely, involves acknowledging and valuing each member's unique strengths, contributions, and viewpoints. It encourages inclusivity, teamwork, and mutual aid. Trust and respect lead to greater team morale, better cooperation, and a stronger commitment to team objectives.

Conflicts, though often viewed as negative, can be beneficial in an Agile environment if managed correctly. They can lead to superior solutions, stimulate creativity, and enhance team dynamics. Agile teams encourage open conversations, where conflicts can be expressed, examined, and addressed promptly. They view conflicts not as personal disputes but as differences over ideas or methods that need to be resolved for the team's advantage. The Scrum Master frequently facilitates these discussions, aiding the team in expressing their opinions, understanding each other's viewpoints, and collaboratively finding solutions. Hence, conflict resolution skills are essential for maintaining a peaceful, productive team environment.

Agile teams function on the concept of distributed leadership. While there are designated roles like the Product Owner and Scrum Master, leadership responsibilities are dispersed among all team members. Each member is empowered to make decisions, take initiative, and be accountable for the team's results. This distributed leadership model eliminates hierarchical obstacles, enhances team ownership, and fosters proactive behavior. It utilizes the diverse strengths and skills within the team, enhancing the team's reactivity, inventiveness, and productivity. Consequently, the team becomes more self-organizing and resilient, able to adapt and flourish in a dynamic, complex environment.

Balancing Power and Decision-making

Agile approaches heavily underscore the importance of elevating the team. Rather than just being inactive implementers of tasks, team members are given authority to make impactful decisions, solve issues, and take comprehensive ownership of their tasks. This elevation fosters a deeper level of involvement and creativity within the team. Team members who experience a sense of empowerment often exhibit more initiative, exhibit a more profound sense of responsibility for their tasks, and are more committed to delivering high-standard results. This can ultimately lead to a boost in productivity and enhancement of product quality.

The Scrum Master's primary duty is to facilitate the Agile process, assisting the team in surmounting obstacles and ensuring that the team sticks to Agile principles and practices. The Product Owner, conversely, acts as the representative of the customer within the team and makes critical decisions regarding the product's priorities. However, these roles are not about authority and control; they underscore service to the team and stakeholders and enable a cooperative decision-making process.

Agile teams are renowned for their joint decision-making process. The team collectively decides on the work scope for each iteration during sprint planning. Similarly, retrospectives provide a chance for the team to jointly reflect on their performance and consent on areas for improvement. This practice of joint decision-making nurtures a common understanding of objectives, fortifies team commitment, and fosters accountability.

Openness is a crucial factor in Agile teams, especially when power and decision-making are dispersed among members. Information pertinent to the project, including the product backlog, sprint progress, performance metrics, and feedback, should be freely accessible to all team members. This openness ensures that everyone has access to the information required to make informed decisions, preventing the accumulation of power and control in the hands of a few.

When power and decision-making are dispersed, disputes are unavoidable. However, Agile teams see these disputes as chances for improvement. They encourage constructive conflict – disagreements that can lead to improved decisions and solutions. The aim is to cultivate a culture of respectful and open conversation and to stay focused on the joint objective of delivering customer value.

Trust is critical for sharing power and decision-making within the team. Trust allows team members to rely on each other, openly express their thoughts, take calculated risks, and commit to their decisions and actions. Trust is built over time through consistent behavior, transparency, shared experiences, and the demonstration of skills and integrity. By building trust, Agile teams can encourage stronger cooperation, resilience, and better performance.

Chapter Four: Agile Ceremonies

Daily standups, often called daily scrums, play a crucial role in Agile frameworks. Their main objective is to serve as a venue for the team to align on the work completed, tasks planned for the day, and any potential hurdles that might stand in the way of progress. By doing this, the team can sustain a regular work pace, referred to as the "sprint rhythm," while simultaneously ensuring open communication among all team members. This recurring alignment fosters teamwork, allows for early identification of potential issues, and makes sure everyone is working towards the shared sprint objectives. It also fortifies the Agile principle of continual self-evaluation on how to increase efficiency and adjust behaviors as necessary.

The daily standup is a brief, concentrated meeting, typically lasting about 15 minutes. To establish a habit, the standup should be held at the same time and place every day. During this meeting, each team member briefly answers three questions:

What did I accomplish yesterday?

What will I work on today?

Are there any impediments in my way?

The standup's format promotes discipline, productivity, and regular communication among team members. However, it's important to remember that the daily standup is not meant to serve as a problem-solving or detailed discussion platform. Any issues requiring a thorough discussion should be addressed in a separate meeting following the standup. This approach ensures the standup remains short and focused, respecting everyone's time and maintaining the meeting's efficiency.

During a daily standup, the Scrum Master takes on the role of a guide. They are responsible for making sure the meeting begins on time, follows the agreed-upon format, and stays within the predetermined time limit. Their function is to steer the conversation, assisting the team to stay focused on addressing the three questions and stepping in if the discussion strays into problem-solving or becomes overly detailed. By preserving the structure and flow of the standup, the Scrum Master supports the team in maximizing the effectiveness of this crucial communication tool.

The daily standup acts as a catalyst for open and straightforward communication among team members. It establishes a space where individuals are encouraged to share their accomplishments, outline their tasks for the day, and highlight any obstacles they may encounter. The aim is to foster an open exchange where each participant can express their individual progress and bring attention to issues that could impede their work. Truthfulness is greatly appreciated, particularly when discussing challenges, as promptly addressing these is crucial for preserving the team's momentum and productivity.

In line with the essence of Agile, daily standups should also serve as a platform for perpetual enhancement. Teams are urged to experiment and adjust the structure, questions asked, or techniques employed within the standup to meet their distinct needs. This might encompass altering the meeting's framework, modifying the way progress is monitored, or revamping how challenges are tackled. The ultimate objective should be to bolster the standup's efficacy as a tool for daily planning, coordination, and problem pinpointing, thus amplifying the overall productivity and cohesion of the team.

For geographically scattered or remote teams, standups can be conducted virtually via a range of video conferencing tools. While the core principles and purpose of the standup persist, running standups in a virtual environment may necessitate additional considerations. For example, efforts should be made to ensure that everyone is actively participating and has the chance to express their thoughts. Moreover, potential challenges like time zone disparities and technical glitches need to be factored in. Tools such as virtual task boards or shared documents can be utilized to keep everyone informed, promoting transparency and upholding the rhythm of the standup in a virtual context.

Sprint Planning

The fundamental aim of sprint planning is to outline a tangible goal for the forthcoming sprint and pinpoint the specific set of tasks from the product backlog the team will undertake to achieve that goal. This session is key in forming a mutual understanding of the team's targets and their dedication to them. Moreover, it sets the stage for the team's collaboration over the next sprint, charting a clear route towards the anticipated results. The outcome of this meeting is a sprint goal and an elaborate sprint backlog, which acts as the team's roadmap for the sprint.

The sprint planning meeting is a joint endeavour that involves the Product Owner, the Scrum Master, and the Development Team.

The Product Owner introduces the views of the users, stakeholders, and the business to the meeting. They are tasked with clarifying the context and objectives of the high-priority product backlog items, and with aiding the team in understanding the value these items will deliver. They steer the team in picking the most valuable and suitable work for the forthcoming sprint.

The Scrum Master presides over the meeting, ensuring the procedure is comprehended and adhered to, that conversations remain targeted and efficient, and that the team arrives at a consensus about the sprint goal and the associated product backlog items.

The Development Team, being the ones who will carry out the work, evaluate the technical feasibility of the proposed work. They determine how much work they can feasibly pledge to in the next sprint, based on their comprehension of their capacity and the complexity of the work.

The sprint planning session is typically split into two stages:

The first stage is devoted to crafting the sprint goal. This goal is a brief statement that encapsulates the mission of the upcoming sprint and offers a collective target that unifies and steers the team's endeavours. This procedure often entails discussions about the highest value items in the product backlog, the team's capacity, the product roadmap, and other factors that could impact the focus of the sprint.

The second stage is about cherry-picking the product backlog items that align with the sprint goal and segmenting them into manageable tasks. This is when the team debates the specifics of how they will deliver each item, which can include technical discussions, risk evaluations, effort estimation, and detailed task generation. This stage ensures that the team has a lucid, shared comprehension of what needs to be accomplished, and produces a transparent action plan for the sprint.

Sprint planning is an event with a set maximum length, or in other words, a time-boxed activity. The Scrum Guide advocates a time-box of up to two hours for each sprint week. So, a two-week sprint would correspond to a planning session that lasts at most four hours. Sticking to this time-box is crucial for maintaining the meeting's focus and efficiency. The time-box prompts attendees to prioritize conversations and aids in avoiding overly detailed discussions or loss of direction. However, it's vital to note that the aim isn't just to use up the time-box, but to accomplish the objectives of the meeting.

The main results of the sprint planning session are a distinctly outlined sprint goal and the sprint backlog. The sprint goal is a concise, high-level aim that the team commits to achieving during the sprint. The sprint backlog is an exhaustive list of tasks, sourced from the product backlog items that the team aims to finalize to attain the sprint goal. This sprint backlog gives the team a detailed itinerary for the sprint, specifying exactly what has to be done, and often, providing recommendations on how to accomplish it.

To ensure a productive sprint planning session, several elements need to be considered:

Well-Refined Product Backlog: A polished product backlog is crucial for an efficient sprint planning meeting. This implies that the items in the backlog should be clearly outlined, comprehended well, and properly prioritized. This aids the team in understanding what work needs completion, its significance, and how it contributes to the overall objectives of the product.

Active Participation: Everyone in the team should actively engage in the meeting. Each member brings a distinct viewpoint, and their contribution is vital for comprehending the work and making a viable commitment.

Open Communication:: Foster transparent communication to make sure everyone has a clear, mutual understanding of the sprint goal, the selected backlog items, and the execution of the work. This involves discussing any risks, assumptions, dependencies, or concerns that could affect the work.

Realistic Commitment: The team should focus on creating a practical and achievable plan for the sprint. This involves understanding the team's capacity, the complexity of the work, and any other factors that could influence the team's ability to deliver. Overcommitting can lead to burnout and diminished quality, while undercommitting can cause overlooked opportunities.

Sprint Review

The Sprint Review is a pivotal event in Scrum, taking place at the conclusion of every sprint. The primary aim of this gathering is to scrutinize the work increment completed during the sprint and to adjust the product backlog according to feedback and lessons learned. The meeting provides a stage for the Scrum team to display their work to the stakeholders, discuss accomplished and pending work, and to gather precious feedback. Additionally, the sprint review is instrumental in re-establishing alignment among the team and stakeholders on the product roadmap, adjusting plans and priorities based on newly acquired insights.

The Sprint Review involves all key Scrum roles and any related stakeholders. The meeting includes the Scrum Master, Product Owner, and the Development Team. Stakeholders—persons or groups who have a stake in the product's result—are also invited to attend.

The Sprint Review has an informal structure, more akin to a cooperative dialogue than a unidirectional presentation. The Product Owner typically steers the meeting. It commences with the Product Owner detailing which items from the product backlog have been finished during the sprint and which haven't. The Development Team then shares their sprint experiences, encompassing the challenges they met and the solutions they discovered.

Subsequently, the Development Team presents the work accomplished during the sprint, letting everyone witness the product increment. Post-demonstration, the Product Owner leads a discussion regarding the product backlog, outlining its status considering the work finalized, stakeholder feedback, and any shifts in the larger context (such as market or organizational changes).

Finally, an inclusive discussion involving all attendees centers around the next moves. This conversation could delve into potential product backlog items for future sprints, technical debt, market shifts, or business priorities. The intention is to use the insights collected during the Sprint Review to guide future planning and decision-making. This practice ensures the team continues to deliver value and that the product develops in a manner consistent with stakeholder needs and business aims.

The Sprint Review's duration is time-boxed and contingent on the sprint's length. For a sprint that lasts a month, the Sprint Review is allocated a maximum of four hours. For shorter sprints, the review should also be accordingly shorter. This method of time-boxing guarantees that discussions maintain focus and don't excessively extend, while still providing ample time for scrutinizing and adjusting the product increment and the product backlog. It fosters active engagement from all attendees in the conversation, encourages the sharing of feedback, and aids the decision-making process about future steps in a time-conscious way.

The primary output of the Sprint Review is an updated product backlog. This modification mirrors any changes or updates derived from the stakeholder feedback and the team's discourse during the Sprint Review. The backlog might comprise updated estimates of effort for existing items, shifts in the priority of items, the inclusion of new items, or the deletion of items no longer relevant. Additionally, the Sprint Review results in a collective understanding among the team and stakeholders about the current status of the product, the progress made during the sprint, and the course for the next sprint. This common understanding is essential for alignment and cooperation in the subsequent tasks.

The Sprint Review is a fundamental component of the Agile development procedure. It embodies the Agile principles of transparency, inspection, and adaptation. The Sprint Review promotes transparency by offering a stage for the team to display their work and for the stakeholders to comprehend the product's progress and the team's performance. It backs inspection by facilitating a thorough discussion about the accomplished work, the challenges encountered, and the feedback from stakeholders. And it fosters adaptation by permitting the team and stakeholders to utilize these insights to adapt the product backlog and adjust the course for the subsequent sprint. Consequently, the Sprint Review contributes to the product and the process's continual enhancement, ensuring that the team stays adaptive and value-oriented.

Sprint Retrospective

The Sprint Retrospective is a specialized event conducted at each sprint's conclusion, allowing the Scrum team to review their methods and design a roadmap for enhancements to be instituted during the succeeding Sprint. This occasion offers a formal avenue for introspection and learning. The team reflects on the just-concluded sprint - evaluating the procedures, interactions, tools, and practices - discussing their successes and shortcomings. They deliberate on both victories and defeats, strengths and weak points, aiming to extract knowledge from their experience. However, retrospection alone isn't sufficient; the team also capitalizes on this occasion to strategize for the future. Drawing on their introspections, they pinpoint actionable enhancements in their work techniques, practices, tools, communication, or any other facet that can augment their efficacy, efficiency, and satisfaction. These enhancements aren't merely theoretical propositions; the team pledges to incorporate them into the next Sprint. Thus, the Sprint Retrospective serves as an engine for continuous, gradual process enhancement and promotes a culture of learning and adaptability.

The Sprint Retrospective is a team event that includes the complete Scrum Team - the Product Owner, the Scrum Master, and the Development Team. The Product Owner contributes insights regarding the product vision, customer requirements, and business objectives. The Development Team members convey their experiences from the field, the technical obstacles, collaboration dilemmas, or process inefficiencies they encountered. The Scrum Master steers the meeting, ensuring a positive, fruitful, and candid environment where every opinion is respected, and every suggestion is contemplated. They also verify that the meeting remains focused, constructive, and culminates in lucid action plans. Every participant is an equal contributor to the dialogue, providing insights, articulating concerns, proposing enhancements, and deciding on the action plans.

While the layout of the Sprint Retrospective can be diversified to keep the meeting appealing and effective, it typically consists of three phases: accumulating insights, examining and conversing, and planning enhancements.

In the initial phase, the team ponders over the sprint, and each member contributes their observations regarding what transpired, what went smoothly, and what didn't. They discuss their experiences, obstacles, triumphs, unexpected events, and learnings. Various techniques like 'Timeline', 'Happiness Metric', or 'Sailboat' can facilitate this data accumulation in an engaging and comprehensive manner.

In the second phase, the team deliberates on the gathered data to discern the inherent patterns, causes, or trends.

They pinpoint the strengths to be amplified and the weaknesses to be remedied. Techniques like '5 Whys', 'Fishbone Diagram', or 'Dot Voting' can facilitate an in-depth examination of the issues and help prioritize them.

In the final phase, the team settles on the improvements. They brainstorm solutions, strategies, or alterations that can tackle the identified problems or enhance their practices. They then choose a few (usually one to three) actionable, quantifiable, and attainable improvement items that they commit to instituting in the next sprint. Tools like 'SMART goals' or 'Impact-Effort Matrix' can aid in this decision-making process.

By adhering to this structured methodology, the team ensures that the Sprint Retrospective isn't merely a discussion forum but yields tangible enhancements.

The primary outcome of the Sprint Retrospective is the identification of concrete improvement steps that the team agrees to implement in the next Sprint. This outcome is often in the form of an actionable plan that details what changes will be made, who will be responsible for implementing them, and how their impact will be measured. These improvements could span a broad range of areas, such as process enhancements, changes in communication or collaboration practices, updates to the team's definition of "Done", adoption of new tools or technologies, or steps to improve team dynamics and morale. The identified improvements are added to the Sprint Backlog of the upcoming Sprint, ensuring that they are treated as priority work items and not lost in the hustle of daily tasks. By documenting and tracking these actions, the team makes a visible commitment to continuous improvement and holds themselves accountable for it.

The Retrospective provides a regular, structured opportunity for the team to reflect on their work methods, learn from their experiences, and proactively seek ways to do better. By making this an integral part of every Sprint, Agile teams ensure that improvement is not a sporadic or reactive effort but a continuous, proactive process. Over time, this leads to a virtuous cycle of learning, adapting, and improving, enabling the team to deliver better results, faster, and with higher satisfaction. Additionally, the emphasis on continuous improvement fosters a growth mindset, encouraging team members to embrace challenges, learn from failures, and continuously strive to increase their skills and capabilities.

Chapter Five: Artifacts

Let's start by taking a closer look at the Product Backlog.

A Product Backlog can be considered a comprehensive inventory of potential modifications, enhancements, alterations, or repairs that could be applied to a product. This inventory, arranged by importance, functions as a planning instrument guiding the team's efforts over time. Product Backlog Items (PBIs), typically formulated as User Stories, each outline a specific attribute or functionality that would offer some value to the end-user or other stakeholders. The Product Backlog is a living document, signifying it adapts and matures throughout the product's life cycle as more knowledge is gained, novel requirements or ideas emerge, and as market or business environments shift. It's crucial to understand that the Product Backlog isn't a rigid agreement or an unalterable plan, but instead a fluid roadmap directing the team towards the product vision while permitting adjustments based on feedback, learning, and changes.

The Product Owner bears the primary responsibility for handling the Product Backlog. This includes maintaining the assortment of Backlog items, scripting and refining the item descriptions to ensure they're lucid and actionable, and arranging the items based on their relevance to the product and business. The Product Owner works in close association with stakeholders, customers, and the development team to confirm that the Backlog mirrors the demands and anticipations of customers, aligns with the strategic trajectory of the product, and is comprehensible by the team. They are also required to continuously review and update the Backlog to accommodate feedback, changes in the market or business strategy, and learning from product development and utilization.

Assigning priority within the Product Backlog is a pivotal duty of the Product Owner. The items in the Backlog are ordered according to their priority, with the items of the utmost importance placed at the top. This sequence establishes the order in which the team will address the items. The prioritization typically depends on a mix of factors, including business value (the influence on users, revenue, or strategic objectives), risk and uncertainty (the extent of the unknown or risk associated with the item), dependencies (the necessity to complete the item before others), and complexity (the effort required by the item). This practice ensures that the team is consistently focusing on the most valuable and critical work at any point in time, optimizing the value delivered in each Sprint. Prioritization is not a one-off task; instead, the Product Owner is required to regularly reevaluate and adjust the priority of Backlog items in response to feedback, progression, and contextual changes.

The fine-tuning of the Product Backlog is an ongoing activity wherein the Product Owner and the Development Team join forces to examine items on the Product Backlog, ensuring they're aptly prepared and sequenced for impending Sprints. During this progression, larger elements may be partitioned into tinier, more manageable pieces, criteria for acceptance are set forth, and the specifics of the upcoming tasks are deliberated and elucidated. The goal is to confirm that items at the summit of the Product Backlog are ripe for selection during a Sprint Planning meeting. These items should ideally be adequately independent, flexible, beneficial, estimable, compact, and verifiable—commonly encapsulated by the mnemonic INVEST. Backlog refinement usually takes up no more than 10% of the Development Team's capacity. Although it's a continual activity, many teams allocate specific intervals for refinement tasks to ensure this essential duty does not fall by the wayside.

User Stories are a prevalent method for expressing Product Backlog items. A User Story registers a requirement from the user's or customer's viewpoint, focusing on the benefit or outcome they wish to accomplish. They're typically articulated in the format: "As a [type of user], I want [an action] so that [a benefit/a value]." This framework keeps the team committed to delivering value to the users and aids them in understanding why a feature or function is beneficial. User Stories are designed to encourage discussion, so they are intentionally left somewhat ambiguous; the finer details are fleshed out in dialogue between the Product Owner and the Development Team. Accompanying each User Story are acceptance criteria, which outline the precise conditions that must be satisfied for the story to be deemed complete.

Estimation in the realm of the Product Backlog pertains to the practice of assigning a comparative measure of effort to each item. This is often done using a metric known as "story points." Story points gauge the effort needed to implement a Product Backlog item, taking into account factors such as the volume of work to do, the complexity of the work, and any risks or uncertainties in the work. The Development Team is accountable for these estimations, which aid in shaping Sprint Planning decisions. During Sprint Planning, the team utilizes these estimates to guide their selection of items from the Product Backlog, determining what they can realistically pledge to accomplish in the forthcoming Sprint. It's crucial to remember that these estimates are not guarantees, but they help provide a benchmark for the team's capacity.

Sprint Backlog

The Sprint Backlog comprises the selection of Product Backlog Items (PBIs) that the team pledges to complete in a Sprint, alongside the strategy for their execution. It is more than a mere list—it depicts the team's projection of the features that will constitute the subsequent Increment and the tasks required to produce that functionality. The Sprint Backlog exists to offer a precise view of the team's undertakings during the Sprint. It serves as a navigation tool, aiding the team in self-organizing their work to align with the Sprint Goal. It delivers transparency around the team's tasks, assists in managing team workload, and instills a sense of accomplishment as tasks are concluded.

The Development Team cherry-picks items from the Product Backlog, grounded in their comprehension of the product, their capabilities, and the Product Owner's preferences. Once items are singled out for the Sprint, the Development Team deconstructs these into tasks. Each task embodies a work unit necessary to carry out the chosen items. These tasks constitute the Sprint Backlog. It's vital to remember that only the Development Team can modify the Sprint Backlog during a Sprint, granting them autonomy and promoting self-organization.

The Sprint Goal is a succinct, clear delineation of what the team aims to accomplish during the Sprint. It's a superordinate objective that instructs the Development Team on the rationale behind the construction of the Increment. It is devised during the Sprint Planning meeting, typically in cooperation with the Product Owner. The Sprint Goal and the chosen Product Backlog items then steer the team in formulating the Sprint Backlog. Throughout the Sprint, the team keeps the Sprint Goal in perspective, and it serves to maintain their efforts focused and unified. The Sprint Goal offers flexibility in terms of the functionality implemented within the Sprint: as long as the Sprint Goal is met, the precise make-up of the Sprint Backlog can vary.

The Sprint Backlog is an evolving entity and is subject to updates and adjustments by the Development Team throughout the Sprint as additional information surfaces. Although the broader Sprint Goal persists, the team's route to achieving that goal can be altered as the Sprint unfolds. For example, tasks might be incorporated, eliminated, or reshaped as the team gains deeper insights into their work. This capacity for adaptation complies with the Agile doctrine of welcoming change, enabling optimal efficiency and effectiveness in realizing the Sprint Goal.

The Sprint Backlog is frequently depicted through resources like a physical board, a digital board, or other Agile project management software. Each task is symbolized, typically on a card or sticky note, and these tasks transition through various stages (such as "to do", "in progress", and "done") as the work proceeds. This visible tracking, also referred to as a Kanban board, permits the team to readily identify what work has been accomplished, what is underway, and what remains to be done. It also fosters transparency and unreserved communication, as all team members and stakeholders can survey the status of the Sprint's tasks instantaneously.

As the Sprint concludes, the objective is to have all items on the Sprint Backlog finalized, culminating in a potentially releasable Increment. However, if any items remain uncompleted, they are usually reevaluated and returned to the Product Backlog. Subsequently, they may be contemplated for future Sprints, but they must traverse the Sprint Planning process once again to be incorporated in a new Sprint. This avoids the rollover of tasks without reconsideration, guaranteeing that priority and team capacity are perpetually considered.

Burndown Charts

What is a Burndown Chart? It is a visual instrument employed in Scrum and other Agile frameworks to illustrate the pace at which tasks are being completed and the remaining work over a given duration. It aids teams in monitoring their progress during a Sprint or a Release and offers insights into how effectively they are sustaining their rhythm to finish their work within the allocated timeline. This capacity enables the team to make necessary adjustments to remain on course. Burndown charts are a potent method to forecast when all tasks will be done.

A Burndown Chart comprises two principal components. The horizontal axis (X-axis) generally signifies time, frequently the days within a Sprint. The vertical axis (Y-axis) symbolizes the outstanding work. This work could be depicted in different units such as story points, hours, or the count of backlog items. The chart commences at the top left, with the total estimated work for the Sprint, and ideally concludes at the bottom right, indicating that all the work has been executed.

The advancement in a Burndown Chart is represented by a line that begins at the top left and trends towards the bottom right. Each point on this line indicates the volume of remaining work at the close of each day. The "burn down" metaphor is derived from the line ideally moving downwards as the team wraps up work, diminishing the amount of work "left to burn". If tasks are accomplished as expected, the line will hit zero by the close of the Sprint, suggesting all planned work has been completed. Divergences from this ideal line can hint that the team is either ahead or lagging, offering an opportunity for the team to promptly address any potential issues.

The Ideal Trend Line within a Burndown Chart is a direct line that extends from the top left corner (the entirety of the work at the Sprint's inception) to the bottom right corner (zero tasks left at the Sprint's conclusion). This line illustrates the anticipated burn rate if tasks were equally shared out and fulfilled at a steady pace across the Sprint. The Ideal Trend Line functions as a visual benchmark that the team can use to gauge their actual progression. Any divergence from this line signifies that the team's advancement isn't as initially strategized, and it enables the team to quickly discern how they are faring against the ideal scenario.

The primary application of a Burndown Chart is to graphically track the evolution of work in a Sprint and to forecast whether the team will be able to accomplish the work by the Sprint's end. The juxtaposition between the actual progression and the Ideal Trend Line allows the team to pinpoint whether they are ahead, on course, or lagging behind their plan. If the actual line is above the ideal line, it suggests the team has more remaining work than anticipated at that juncture in the Sprint, insinuating they are behind schedule. If the actual line is beneath the ideal line, the team is ahead of schedule, having finished more work than anticipated by that stage.

The Burndown Chart is renewed at the closure of each working day, depicting the remaining volume of work after finished tasks have been "burned down". This consistent renewal embodies the Agile principles of transparency, inspection, and adjustment. By renewing and examining the chart daily, the team can promptly react to changes and modify their plan if necessary, making it an invaluable instrument for maintaining cognizance and enabling adaptability in the development procedure. The ongoing visualization aids the team in inspecting their pace, spotting any potential issues or bottlenecks, and implementing corrective measures to stay on track.

Increment

In Agile methodologies, an increment is the aggregation of all the product backlog items finished during a sprint, amalgamated with the output of all previous sprints. Essentially, the increment serves as a progress marker towards the full realization of the end product vision or solution, offering a substantial and tactile representation of the team's advancement. Crafting an increment at the end of each sprint affirms the Agile principle of frequent delivery of functional software, subsequently allowing for consistent product validation, regular and early feedback from stakeholders, and iterative refinement grounded in this feedback. This method can augment product quality, hasten the product's launch, and elevate stakeholder satisfaction.

An increment is meant to be "possibly deployable," signifying that it should meet the usability criteria and align with the team's Definition of Done (DoD). The DoD constitutes a communal understanding within the team concerning the standards that must be fulfilled for the work to be deemed complete. This could incorporate facets such as coding norms, testing specifications, documentation requirements, and integration needs. Nonetheless, a possibly deployable state doesn't always imply that the increment will be instantly dispatched to the end-users upon completion. The choice to release an increment, influenced by factors such as business tactics, market situations, user readiness, or other considerations, is the responsibility of the Product Owner.

The method of developing the product in increments allows Agile teams to ensure that the product always maintains a usable, potentially dispatchable state. This strategy substantially mitigates risks tied to traditional long-term projects, such as unexpected integration challenges, creeping changes in requirements (scope creep), and deviations from the original objective. By frequently delivering potentially deployable increments, teams can garner quicker feedback from stakeholders, validate their presumptions, verify alignment with user needs and market conditions, and recalibrate the product direction or development approach based on the feedback and insights acquired. Hence, incremental development boosts adaptability, ensures ongoing enhancement, and heightens the likelihood of delivering a product that fulfills user needs and offers value.

The practice of working in increments strengthens the three pillars of empirical process control in Scrum: transparency, inspection, and adaptation. Every increment offers a clear, tangible snapshot of the progress made, fostering a shared comprehension of the product's present condition among all involved parties. This facilitates frequent scrutiny of the product, the work performed, and the employed development strategies. Stakeholders have the opportunity to engage with the product features, the team can evaluate the quality and usefulness of their work, and any departures from the anticipated results or potential issues can be caught early. These inspections can drive necessary adaptations, such as refining product backlog items, modifying the development methodology, or even altering the product direction. This continuous cycle of transparency, inspection, and adaptation minimizes risks, promotes ongoing learning and improvement, and enhances the likelihood of addressing user needs and delivering value.

The increment is the focal point of the Sprint Review, an event that concludes each sprint and involves the Scrum team and stakeholders inspecting the increment. The development team showcases the completed work, and the Product Owner clarifies what has been accomplished and what remains undone. Stakeholders offer feedback based on their interaction with the increment and their evolving requirements or market circumstances. This mutual inspection and feedback process helps everyone to comprehend the current state of the product, the value delivered, and any existing gaps or potential enhancements. The Product Owner can utilize this feedback to adjust the product backlog, reorder items, introduce new items, or refine the existing ones. This process ensures the product development stays in sync with user needs, business objectives, and market realities.

It's crucial to highlight that a team can generate multiple increments within a single sprint. Each product backlog item that meets the Definition of Done can be viewed as an increment. These increments collectively contribute to the overall progress and value of the product. This method allows for more frequent inspections and feedback, and also offers more chances to deliver value to the users within a sprint. For instance, should the Product Owner deem it beneficial, and if it aligns with the business strategy, they could release certain increments to the users before the sprint's conclusion, thereby expediting value delivery.

Chapter Six: Agile Planning and Estimation

Let's start with User Stories. User Stories serve as the foundation of every Agile project. Essentially, they are brief, straightforward explanations of a feature, narrated from the viewpoint of the user who desires this new capability. User Stories are crafted in such a way that emphasizes user value, thus keeping the user at the heart of the discussion. A User Story usually follows the template: "As a [type of user], I want [some goal] so that [some reason]." This structure ensures that the User Story revolves around the user, explicitly outlines their aim, and provides a rationale for the request, often indicating the benefit they hope to gain.

The INVEST for User Stories: INVEST is an acronym for Independent, Negotiable, Valuable, Estimable, Small, and Testable - these are characteristics that a well-structured user story should possess. Independent suggests that each user story should stand alone and could be developed in any order. Negotiable relates to the specifics of the work that can be adjusted and decided during development. Valuable signifies that every user story should deliver value to the final user. Estimable implies that it should be feasible to estimate the effort needed to develop the story. Small indicates that user stories should be small enough to be implemented within a single sprint. Lastly, Testable denotes that each user story should be precise enough to be tested.

Acceptance criteria form a crucial aspect of Agile software development as they determine the scope of a user story and are utilized to verify when a story is finished and operating as expected. They consist of a set of pre-established requirements that must be fulfilled for a user story to be accepted by the product owner or user. These requirements are expressed in a way that clearly defines the functionality, behavior, and performance anticipated from the feature. Acceptance criteria are distinct for each user story and outline what the team should accomplish, how a specific feature could be used, under what conditions, and what the outcome should be.

Acceptance Criteria determine what the deliverables will be by outlining the conditions that the software needs to meet for the User Story to be deemed finished. By explaining what the system is expected to do, how it should perform, and any regulations connected to its operation, Acceptance Criteria aid in removing vagueness from requirements. They also lay the groundwork for system testing, acting as reference points for validating a system's functionality.

The creation of Acceptance Criteria is pivotal to the successful realization of User Stories. Well-crafted Acceptance Criteria should be unambiguous, succinct, and comprehensible. They should illustrate the system's performance, not how the solution is employed. They should be articulated in plain language that all stakeholders can grasp, and they must be testable. Testability indicates that it should be feasible to formulate a test based on the criteria, which, if passed, signifies that the Acceptance Criteria have been met. Moreover,

Acceptance Criteria should not be excessively lengthy or complex; if they are, it typically suggests that the User Story needs to be subdivided into smaller segments.

Whereas a User Story offers a broad summary of a feature from the end user's viewpoint, its corresponding Acceptance Criteria supply the precise details that outline the functionality, behavior, and performance of that feature. The User Story sets the context and supplies background, while the Acceptance Criteria dive into the particulars and offer clear definitions of success. They serve as a conduit between the user's need (User Story) and the solution (Acceptance Criteria), empowering the development team to understand and execute the requirements precisely and thoroughly.

Estimation Techniques

Planning Poker, is a group consensus technique employed by Agile teams to gauge the effort necessary to complete user stories or assignments. The activity commences with a user story or task introduced to the group. Every team member, commonly excluding the Scrum Master and Product Owner, proposes an independent estimate of the necessary effort by choosing a card from a pack, each card representing a degree of effort (frequently in terms of time, complexity, or story points). The cards are laid face down, and once all estimates are ready, they're disclosed simultaneously. This practice avoids the likelihood of team members influencing others' estimates. In case of a significant difference between estimates, a discussion is initiated to comprehend different viewpoints, and the process is repeated until an agreement is reached.

T-Shirt Sizes is an estimation technique where work elements, like user stories or tasks, are sorted into different sizes - generally XS (Extra Small), S (Small), M (Medium), L (Large), and XL (Extra Large). This approach is a form of relative estimation that departs from the specificities of time-based estimates and emphasizes more on comparing the relative dimensions of different tasks. This method can streamline the estimation procedure and is handy when a team is novice to Agile methods or when they struggle with overthinking or exactness in their estimates. Once tasks are allocated to different sizes, those that land into larger categories can be further subdivided, if necessary, into smaller, more feasible tasks.

The Bucket System is a swift, relative estimation technique beneficial for estimating a vast number of items in a brief duration. Instead of allotting distinct numbers to each work item, items are compiled into different "containers" or categories that signify ranges of sizes. Each container symbolizes a spectrum of effort or complexity, rather than a distinct value. Work items are discussed one after the other, and each item is assigned to a container that corresponds to a level of effort or size. The items within a single container don't have to be exactly similar in size but are deemed close enough to be assembled together. This technique is especially valuable for executing initial high-level estimates of a large backlog of items.

Dot Voting, occasionally referred to as 'Dotmocracy', is a straightforward strategy for arranging tasks in order of priority or reaching consensus in group decisions. During a Dot Balloting exercise, each participant is given a specified number of dots or votes, which they can allocate among a range of choices, tasks, or ideas presented. The distribution can be decided by the voter – all votes on a single item, one vote on each item, or any other mix. Once every participant has assigned their dots, the votes are tallied, and the items with the majority votes are prioritized. This method enables democratic decision-making, guaranteeing that every opinion is considered. It comes in handy particularly when the team needs to figure out which items should be given immediate attention from a comprehensive list of choices or tasks.

The **Fibonacci Sequence** (1, 2, 3, 5, 8, 13, 21, and so forth) is regularly employed for effort approximation in Agile methodologies. The progression is renowned for its characteristic that each number is the total of the two preceding ones. In the Agile context, this increasing progression encapsulates the concept that the uncertainty and intricacy linked with a task amplify as its magnitude increases. Using Fibonacci numbers for estimations assists teams in sidestepping the trap of presuming false precision for larger and more intricate items. For instance, it recognizes that there's not much tangible difference between a task estimated as requiring 20 days and one estimated at 21 days, despite the evident precision of these figures.

Release and Sprint Planning

Product Release Planning is a critical process within Agile methodologies, providing teams with a roadmap towards the completion of a specific product version or increment. The chief aim of product release planning is to generate a broader perspective of the product's functionalities and features and determine a delivery timeline.

- Product Vision and Objectives: The initial phase of release planning entails defining the overarching vision and objectives of the product. This step is typically conducted with stakeholders and pinpoints the core functionalities and what the product seeks to accomplish.

- Prioritization of Features: Following the clarification of vision and objectives, features are then ranked in order of importance, considering their value to both the business and its customers. This process is usually performed using a strategy such as the MoSCoW method (Must, Should, Could, Won't) or the Value vs. Effort matrix.

- Effort Estimation: Post the prioritization of features, effort prediction is done to estimate the work required to deliver these features. It often includes breaking down the features into smaller, more manageable tasks and estimating the effort using methodologies like Planning Poker or T-Shirt Sizes.

- Release Timeline: Once the effort has been forecasted, a release timeline can be assembled. This timeline stipulates when each feature or group of features will be delivered, essentially providing a roadmap for the project.

The **Sprint Planning** session initiates with a review of the product backlog. The Product Owner explains the backlog items to the Development Team, and an in-depth discussion on each item is held to ensure everyone comprehends what is expected.

- Prioritizing User Stories: The Product Owner, with input from the Development Team, arranges the user stories according to their business value. The goal here is to identify the most valuable user stories to be developed in the forthcoming Sprint.

- User Story Estimation: Subsequently, the Development Team estimates the effort required to complete each user story. Estimation techniques, for example, Planning Poker, may be utilized to ensure that the team reaches an agreement on the required effort.

- Sprint Commitment: Based on the prioritized user stories and their estimations, the Development Team makes a promise on what they believe can be accomplished in the upcoming Sprint. This set of committed user stories forms the Sprint Backlog.

Release Planning and Sprint Planning form two pivotal components in Agile project management. However, their function, scope, and granularity vary.

Release Planning is a macro-level strategy that outlines the main features or capabilities that the end product will possess. This course of action usually spans several months or could even last a year, contingent on the product's intricacy. The primary objective of Release Planning is to lay out a strategic vision of what tasks the team will tackle in the future. This includes pinpointing crucial features, gauging their complexity, aligning them with business preferences, and slotting them into distinct releases. The Release Plan morphs into a roadmap, directing the project's overall trajectory, thereby offering stakeholders an unambiguous glimpse of the product's progression.

Conversely, Sprint Planning is a minutely detailed, short-term strategizing process. At this juncture, which typically recurs every two to four weeks, the team decides the specific tasks they will undertake for the upcoming sprint. They segment the features allocated to the sprint from the Release Plan into manageable jobs and clarify the prerequisites for each task. Sprint Planning consequently contributes to the operational facet of project management, ensuring that the team possesses a lucid, in-depth work scheme for the next few weeks.

Despite their differences, Release Planning and Sprint Planning are interlinked. The overarching Release Plan steers the precise strategies crafted during each Sprint Planning assembly. In this manner, the duo of planning methods collaboratively aligns the team's tasks with the product's strategic trajectory.

Proper Release and Sprint planning offer a host of advantages that aid in the successful realization of a product. Thanks to thorough strategizing, every team member has a clear understanding of what needs to be done, by whom, and when. This eradicates confusion, miscommunication, and inefficiencies during the project's implementation.

Efficient planning ensures that every person involved in the project, from team members to stakeholders, has insight into what the team is tackling and the rationale behind it. This fosters trust, bolsters collaboration, and cultivates accountability.

Proficient planning facilitates every task and feature's alignment with the holistic product vision and business goals. This guarantees that every fragment of work meaningfully contributes to the product's success and the company's strategic targets.

In Agile, strategies are perceived as dynamic documents that should adapt based on fresh data, client feedback, and changes in the business milieu. If a feature doesn't perform as anticipated, if the client's requirements change, or if a superior solution emerges, the plan should be modified accordingly.

This doesn't insinuate that strategizing is futile—far from it. A strategy offers a starting point and a strategic orientation. But it's also anticipated that the strategy will be polished and enhanced as the team gains more insights. This equilibrium between strategizing and adaptability permits the Agile team to consistently deliver optimal value to the customer, refining the product with each cycle based on authentic feedback and shifting conditions.

Tracking Progress and Velocity

Keeping an eye on advancement offers a lucid snapshot of the project's current position and what remains to be accomplished. This clarity enables teams to supervise their tasks more effectively and tweak their approaches as required.

A Cumulative Flow Diagram (CFD) exhibits the status of tasks over time, displaying the quantity of tasks in each phase at any given moment. The diagram consists of several colored bands, each representing a different stage of the process. By scrutinizing the breadth of these bands, the team can detect bottlenecks (where tasks accumulate) and tackle them.

In Scrum, velocity is a parameter that denotes the volume of work a team can execute during a single sprint. It is measured by adding up the points (or sizes) of all fully accomplished user stories or tasks at the sprint's end. The "points" are typically decided during the sprint planning meeting, where the team estimates the effort required for each user story.

After several sprints, the team can compute an average velocity, which offers invaluable data for future strategizing. This average is derived from the team's actual performance, as opposed to speculative estimates, making it a trustworthy metric for planning. For example, if a team's average velocity across the past few sprints is 30 story points, they can reasonably anticipate completing approximately 30 story points worth of work in the subsequent sprint.

Velocity is specific to each team and mirrors the team's unique dynamics, competencies, and working style. Hence, it should not be utilized to compare the performances of different teams—it's not a contest but a planning instrument.

Additionally, velocity is not fixed. Changes in team structure, project prerequisites, or even the growth of team members' skills can influence velocity. Therefore, it's crucial to frequently reassess velocity and adapt sprint planning as needed.

While observing progress and velocity offers crucial insights, there are potential hazards teams should be cognizant of. A common blunder is to become excessively fixated on these metrics at the cost of delivering value. For example, a team might hasten to complete tasks to achieve a high velocity, compromising the quality of their output.

Keep in mind, the primary objective of an Agile project is not to maximize velocity or perfectly stick to estimates—it's to produce a valuable product that satisfies the customer's needs. Metrics like progress observation and velocity are tools designed to assist in this goal, not goals in themselves. They should guide the team's work, not control it.

Chapter Seven: Quality Assurance in Agile

Test-Driven Development (TDD) presents a unique method in software creation, flipping the conventional order of coding followed by testing. With TDD, the emphasis is on devising tests right from the outset.

Red: TDD's journey commences with the "Red" stage, where a test that's set to fail is scripted. This test represents an anticipated enhancement or a fresh capability. This phase underscores the fact that the current code lacks the said feature or functionality. The failed test serves as a compass, indicating the direction in which the development should proceed.

Green: Transitioning to the "Green" stage, the aim for developers narrows down to crafting the minimum necessary code to transition the test from its failed (red) state to a successful (green) one. At this juncture, achieving perfection in the code isn't the focus. The pivotal goal is to rectify the test outcome from red to green as directly and swiftly as possible.

Refactor: After ensuring the test's success, it's time for the "Refactor" stage. In this phase, the coder fine-tunes the written code, excising any redundancies and ensuring the code matches the expected quality benchmarks. The primary aim here is to uphold the functionality while enhancing the code's efficiency and longevity.

Among the top merits of TDD is the promise of superior code reliability. Starting with a test means that every coded segment is intentional, meeting a specific need and adhering to a set standard.

Due to heightened code reliability and thorough testing, the entire code structure is sturdier. This sturdiness implies reduced errors and inconsistencies, making long-term upkeep straightforward and less resource-intensive.

If an error does arise in a TDD environment, the collection of tests functions as a troubleshoot guide. By initiating these tests, developers can pinpoint the origin of the discrepancy, facilitating a faster and more efficient rectification process.

The quick feedback mechanism of TDD is a boon for developers. Testing immediately post-coding offers a real-time evaluation, letting developers ascertain the code's efficacy, thereby promoting swift modifications and enhancements.

One of the biggest misconceptions about TDD is pigeonholing it as merely a testing strategy. While testing remains integral, TDD's essence lies in software structuring and design. The initial test formulation pushes developers to contemplate profoundly about the software's framework, the user interfaces, and the interplay between various elements.

At a glance, it might seem that drafting tests could introduce delays and hamper the development pace. But that's a myopic perspective. In a broader context, TDD might expedite the development phase. Investing time in testing initially can circumvent prolonged hours otherwise expended on untangling intricate issues or redressing challenges emanating from flawed architecture at later stages. The routine feedback mechanism also ensures developers stay aligned, evading substantial alterations.

Implementing TDD

To embark on the TDD journey, the initial step involves choosing a fitting testing framework that aligns with your project's unique requirements. Your selection is typically influenced by various determinants like your chosen programming language, the intended platform, and any special prerequisites of your application. For instance, while JUnit is a go-to for Java aficionados, JavaScript practitioners might lean towards Jasmine or Mocha. A suitable testing framework equips you with essential tools and guidelines to proficiently script, structure, and implement tests.

Initiate with a Test: Central to TDD is this principle. Prior to delving into the actual coding, you need to delineate the anticipated result of a particular function or attribute. This demands a comprehension of its stipulations and crafting a test to ascertain the presumed behavior. This method effectively lays out an objective or benchmark that your subsequent code must fulfill. Naturally, the test will fall short initially, which is both anticipated and acceptable.

During application development, the focus isn't solely on clearing the most recent test. Every fresh code insertion or alteration mandates a comprehensive test run. Adopting this regimen verifies that recent modifications haven't inadvertently derailed or compromised existing features. This continual testing ethos bolsters assurance in the unified functionality of the system.

Simply clearing a test isn't the culmination. Perhaps you've expedited code to turn the test outcome positive, but is your code streamlined? Is its interpretation straightforward? Is it congruent with best practices? Post-test clearance, it's prudent to evaluate the code. Make enhancements wherever deemed fit, ensuring that subsequent changes don't negate the test results. This cyclical method of test-enhance-test guarantees the consistent caliber of your codebase.

Challenges and Pitfalls

A recurrent misstep in TDD is an excessive emphasis on unit tests, which assess discrete software segments separately. Despite their significance, unit tests can't spotlight challenges that manifest when different segments converge. A disproportionate dependency on unit tests could lead to testing blind spots, omitting potential glitches emerging in integration or comprehensive system tests. Hence, unit tests should be harmonized with diverse testing modes for a comprehensive testing strategy.

Any novel strategy or procedure brings an introductory phase of acclimatization. For neophytes to TDD, comprehending test structuring, pinpointing apt testing frameworks, or even internalizing TDD's core tenets might be challenging. This phase can momentarily decelerate the developmental pace. Nevertheless, sustained effort, perseverance, and apt guidance can aid teams in navigating this phase, harnessing TDD's enduring advantages.

Despite the pivotal role of testing, there lurks the risk of overindulgence. Obsessing over granular test details can be counterintuitive. The essence lies in achieving equilibrium — concentrating on evaluating pivotal processes and functions, ensuring the tests are genuinely beneficial and aren't just a statistical play.

TDD transcends mere testing; it revolutionizes the developer's coding perspective. Transitioning from "script now, assess later" to "assess initially, script subsequently" can pose challenges, particularly for practitioners well-versed in time-honored developmental paradigms. This transformation demands a blend of adept training, hands-on practice, and a deep-seated appreciation of TDD's merits.

Pair Programming

Stemming from the methodologies of Extreme Programming (XP) and holding an esteemed spot in the Agile toolkit, Pair Programming unfolds with two developers collaboratively laboring at a single workstation. This duo consists of the "driver" - the one actively penning the code, and the "observer" or "navigator" - meticulously scrutinizing each code fragment. Through this, the technique promotes teamwork, exchange of expertise, and a surge in code standards.

The Driver, engrossed in the act of coding, bridges thoughts into tangible lines of code, navigating the immediate coding challenges. Conversely, the Navigator, although less engaged in direct coding, zooms out to perceive the overarching strategy. This role involves the continuous assessment of the evolving code, ensuring its alignment with design blueprints, compliance with best practices, and vigilance against potential glitches. While the Driver zeroes in on the intricate coding details, the Navigator, by virtue of their position, embraces a holistic view, becoming an indispensable counterpart.

The fluidity of pair programming endorses periodic interchange of roles. This could be time-bound or task-dependent. This rotation ensures sustained enthusiasm and involvement from both programmers, bestowing upon them opportunities to oscillate between granular and macroscopic viewpoints, enriching the code journey.

Advantages

The tandem effort ensures a vigilant watch over the code, flagging potential errors in their infancy. Collective brainstorming often translates to refined and effective solutions.

The ongoing discourse during the coding process naturally leads to the swapping of insights, methodologies, and exemplary practices. Such interactions mitigate knowledge bottlenecks and champion an ethos of perpetual learning.

For seasoned developers, pair programming presents a golden chance to guide their less-experienced counterparts.

This proximity-driven approach offers budding developers a treasure trove of tactics and best practices, a step beyond conventional learning pathways.

The Navigator's real-time code oversight often negates the need for subsequent detailed code assessments, streamlining the developmental cadence.

Confronted with convoluted coding challenges, the presence of a partner offers emotional reinforcement, diluting stress, and fostering a spirit of unity.

Challenges

On the outset, deploying dual developers for a singular code segment may seem resource-heavy. While there's an undeniable initial outlay linked to pair programming, many champion the long-term gains in code quality, diminished debugging durations, and team evolution as worthy trade-offs.

Harmonious collaboration isn't a given. Divergent coding ethos, solution strategies, or elemental interpersonal dynamics might be stumbling blocks. To circumnavigate this, teams might have to trial multiple pair alignments, discovering synergistic duos. Proactive communication tools and conflict navigation strategies can also come to the rescue.

The immersive essence of pair programming, marked by relentless code dissections and debates, can sap mental energies. Recognizing when to hit pause is paramount.

Periodic respites, however brief, can rejuvenate focus and drive, ensuring productive pair programming stints.

Making Pair Programming Work

The efficacy of pair programming isn't solely anchored in methodology; the physical workspace is a paramount component. Considering that a duo of developers will cohabit this space for sustained durations, creating a setting that blends comfort with functionality is indispensable. Employing a vast display or a dual-monitor configuration can enhance code visibility for both parties. A spacious desk to house dual keyboards, mice, and essential peripherals is non-negotiable. Chairs that prioritize ergonomics can alleviate the fatigue of prolonged sessions. Plus, selecting a niche away from bustling corridors or auditory disturbances will ensure undivided attention to the coding endeavor.

Beyond code excellence, pair programming also champions team augmentation and expertise dispersion. Periodically reshuffling the pairs infuses the setup with novelty, ensuring that the routine doesn't stagnate. More crucially, this rotational approach dismantles knowledge bunkers, paving the way for a more holistic team enlightenment. As rotations progress, team members become privy to diverse coding philosophies, resolution approaches, and exemplary practices.

The bedrock of a seamless pair programming experience lies in unhindered communication, underscored by mutual reverence. Owing to the intimate nature of this collaborative venture, occasional discords are par for the course. Yet, navigating these with an inclusive mindset and an appetite for comprehension is vital. Both coders should find ease in vocalizing their methodologies, probing quandaries, and partaking in constructive critique. A culture rooted in bilateral respect transforms these occasional frictions into rich learning avenues.

Pair Programming in a Remote World

With the ascendancy of remote work, pair programming's traditional blueprint has undergone necessary recalibrations.

The digital revolution has made remote pair programming not just feasible but also streamlined. Solutions like Visual Studio Code's Live Share empower coders to jointly craft and troubleshoot code, transcending geographical confines. Synchronized coding, shared terminals, and joint debugging sessions echo the ambiance of physical pair programming. Another utility, tmate, is a boon for disseminating terminal interactions, proving invaluable for backend troubleshooting or non-GUI contexts.

Even as utilities like Live Share facilitate code collaboration, the intrinsic human rapport remains pivotal. Video engagement platforms, such as Zoom or Microsoft Teams, come to the fore here. Deciphering a partner's non-verbal cues adds layers to the conversation, enriching the dialogue. The visual connection also emulates the engagement intensity of co-located pairing, ensuring sustained immersion from both ends. Uninterrupted vocal exchanges breathe life into the virtual pair programming model.

Continuous Integration/Continuous Delivery (CI/CD)

Continuous Integration, commonly abbreviated as CI, encapsulates a developmental approach where developers routinely converge their code alterations into a unified repository. Each time this amalgamation occurs, the introduced changes are subjected to automatic builds and assessments. This habitual amalgamation and verification model aims to swiftly identify integration anomalies, thus assuring that the software remains operationally viable.

One notable benefit of CI is its rapid feedback mechanism. The moment a developer consolidates their code alterations, the automated apparatus springs into action, orchestrating builds and evaluations. Consequently, if discrepancies or glitches emerge, they are instantly pinpointed, permitting developers to rectify them while the relevant details are still top of mind.

By subjecting each consolidation to systematic tests, CI ascertains that the software's caliber remains unwavering. This method aids in thwarting the accumulation of "subpar code", safeguarding the software's integrity over the long haul.

Given the recurring nature of integration, the magnitude of concurrent code mergers is relatively diminutive. This facilitates simpler glitch detection and resolution, curtails integration snags, and diminishes the odds of intricate merge confrontations.

Continuous Delivery (CD)

Often perceived as the natural progression of CI, Continuous Delivery, abbreviated as CD, is a methodology ensuring that every software alteration, post its successful CI scrutiny, remains primed for deployment. It refines the concluding phases of the release blueprint, guaranteeing that software is poised for a swift and trustworthy release when needed.

An adept CD conduit ensures a fluid transition from code commitment to deployment. This trims down the release intervals, empowering entities to swiftly usher in enhancements, updates, or rectifications.

With a profound emphasis on procedural automation, CD curtails human-induced inaccuracies, paving the way for more robust rollouts. This perpetual feedback mechanism fortifies product excellence.

CD mandates that software perpetually remains in a deploy-ready state. This strategic leverage grants organizations the latitude to define their release timelines based on business imperatives rather than binding tech stipulations, thus aligning with market dynamics.

Implementing CI/CD

It's imperative that every facet of a project, encompassing application scripts, infrastructure blueprints, or setups, be archived in a version oversight system, for instance, Git. This nurtures an organized milieu conducive for tracking transitions, fostering collaboration, and facilitating rollbacks when warranted.

Through test automation, squads can ascertain that every introduced alteration stands up to potential backslides. This diminishes dependency on hands-on assessments, which often are susceptible to oversights and are resource-intensive.

Instead of resorting to hands-on compilation and assembly of apps, codifying this progression assures a uniform and reproducible build trajectory. Instrumentalities such as Jenkins, CircleCI, or Travis CI can be instrumental in architecting these automated build arteries.

For CD, utilities like Jenkins, Spinnaker, or AWS CodeDeploy can mechanize the rollout phase, confirming that software is methodically and uniformly propagated across diverse scenarios.

After deployment, it's pivotal to perpetually oversee applications utilizing platforms like Datadog, Splunk, or Prometheus. This endows squads with the capability to expeditiously identify, rectify, and extrapolate from any operational hurdles, cementing a perpetually vibrant feedback cycle.

CI/CD in the Software Development Lifecycle (SDLC)

The Software Development Lifecycle (SDLC) denotes a structured approach encompassing the phases of conceptualizing, designing, verifying, rolling out, and sustaining software applications. Continuous Integration and Continuous Deployment/Delivery (CI/CD) meld effortlessly into this journey, presenting a refined paradigm to conceive, validate, and launch software.

Central to CI is the principle of routine code amalgamations. Instead of developers toiling individually and converging alterations after extended intervals, CI advocates several integrations within a day. Such recurrent unifications prompt automatic compilations and evaluations, certifying that every novel code segment aligns harmoniously with the prevailing foundation and achieves the anticipated caliber thresholds.

Advancing from CI, Continuous Delivery ascertains that post the clearance of automated assessments, modifications are perpetually prepped for manual deployment to the live environment. This strategy guarantees a fluid and uniform transition of alterations from conception to live deployment.

An evolved derivative of Continuous Delivery ensures that every modification, post clearing the automated checks, isn't just primed for deployment but is indeed automatically launched to the live environment. This blueprint autonomously governs the rollout mechanism, ensuring users receive updates in the shortest possible timespan.

Tools & Technologies

The CI/CD domain is expansive, inhabited by a plethora of instruments fashioned to aid every segment of the conduit:

Version Control: These utilities archive and oversee codebase transitions. Examples: Git stands as a decentralized versioning system, whereas venues like GitHub and Bitbucket provide cloud-centric repositories coupled with team collaboration utilities.

Integration & Build Tools: These expedite the Continuous Integration phase, digitizing the compilation and verification procedures. Illustrations: Jenkins dominates as a prevalent open-source utility, while Travis CI and CircleCI cater with cloud-centric remedies.

Containerization: Containers encapsulate an app alongside all its requisite elements, delivering consistent platforms. Illustration: Docker.

Orchestration: These instruments supervise and digitize the launch, amplification, and management of container-encapsulated applications. Illustration: Kubernetes.

Deployment: Utilities specialized in digitizing the rollout mechanism, vouching for uniform and dependable releases. Illustrations: Ansible for setup management and Spinnaker for extensive cloud continuous delivery.

Monitoring: After the rollout, these instruments persistently oversee applications, registering efficiency and identifying anomalies. Illustrations: Grafana and Prometheus for open-source oversight, and New Relic for app efficiency tracking.

Challenges & Considerations

Integration and sustenance of a CI/CD paradigm come with their own set of challenges.

Embarking on a CI/CD journey transcends mere tool adoption; it symbolizes a profound metamorphosis in team dynamics. It necessitates intensified synergy among squads, an anticipatory strategy to challenges, collective accountabilities, and an appetite for swift feedback cycles.

Erecting a resilient CI/CD conduit isn't an overnight achievement. It demands meticulous strategizing, tool adjudication, and configuration choreography. This preliminary commitment in terms of duration and assets can occasionally weigh heavily.

A CI/CD conduit doesn't operate on an "install and overlook" philosophy. As utilities mature, security loopholes appear, and the software undergoes transformations, periodic refurbishments and sustenance become pivotal to ascertain that the conduit retains its potency, security, and efficacy.

Dealing with Bugs and Technical Debt

In the sphere of software development, two challenges frequently stand out: bugs and technical debt. These two elements unexpectedly drop in, often lingering longer than desired, clouding the clarity of our digital designs. Addressing these concerns goes beyond mere coding—it involves a strategic dance between immediate requirements and enduring viability.

Technical debt is essentially the price tagged on immediate but possibly short-sighted decisions. It's analogous to acquiring a loan: while software might be crafted quicker, as with all debts, there's accruing interest. This accumulating interest reveals itself as growing challenges when it comes to the upkeep and evolution of the software. Similar to how monetary obligations can destabilize a firm if left unchecked, neglected technical debt has the potential to risk the durability and vitality of a software initiative.

The roots of technical debt are diverse. Occasionally, it arises from a deliberate choice, favoring expedience over flawlessness. At other times, it's the result of unpredicted intricacies or evolving needs. Then, there's the perpetually shifting tech domain, where what's regarded as revolutionary today might be seen as antiquated tomorrow.

Dealing with bugs pertains to addressing those unplanned and surprising software missteps. Although they might coincide with technical debt, they aren't identical twins. Bugs stand out as immediate glitches demanding swift action. In contrast, technical debt has a more enduring nature. It may not always shout its presence, but its persistent influence might gradually weaken the software's core foundations.

To manage bugs and technical debt effectively, a few strategies are paramount:

Regularly Allocate Time for Refactoring

Fundamentally, refactoring revolves around enhancing the inner configuration of code without altering its outward functionality. It's akin to decluttering a messy room; the contents don't change, but they're now organized in a more logical and easily navigable way.

Analogous to a home needing routine upkeep to stay habitable, software needs refactoring to stay easily manageable. With the evolution of the software, as fresh features integrate and bugs get rectified, the code might turn messy, repetitive, or obsolete. Refactoring rectifies these complications, guaranteeing the software's continuous robustness.

Habitual refactoring can result in more understandable code, diminished bug occurrences, effortless upkeep, and expedited future development. By consistently tidying up, teams can restrain the growth of technical debt, streamlining the process of instilling updates or expansions in the software.

Refactoring isn't random. It's a systematic endeavor steered by industry-recognized norms and guidelines. It comprises activities such as decluttering intricate procedures, rebranding variables for lucidity, segmenting expansive classes, or transitioning from archaic coding norms to contemporary, streamlined ones.

Prioritize Bugs Based on Impact and Frequency

Within any software, bugs might span from trivial visual inconsistencies to critical operational failures. Their repercussions and recurrence rates can vary significantly.

A prevalent technique in software development is deploying the bug intensity matrix. This tool classifies bugs based on their impact (effect on users) and recurrence rate (frequency of manifestation). For instance, an infrequent but devastating bug (like compromising data) would receive immediate attention.

Discerning which bugs warrant urgent redressal versus those that can wait for scheduled upkeep allows development brigades to distribute resources judiciously, directing their endeavors where they're indispensable.

Ranking bug rectifications based on their influence and recurrence guarantees fewer user disturbances, fostering a seamless, dependable software interaction.

Document Decisions Leading to Technical Debt

Occasionally, due to looming deadlines, resource scarcity, or other imminent challenges, brigades might resort to shortcuts during the software development trajectory. While these makeshift solutions might provide temporary relief, they can snowball into 'technical debt', indicating future repercussions stemming from today's makeshift strategies.

When such verdicts materialize, chronicling them becomes paramount. This record should encapsulate the rationale behind the shortcut, immediate anticipated advantages, prospective long-term repercussions, and any potential hazards linked with the judgment.

This chronicle operates as a compass for subsequent software developers. It equips them with backstory, enlightening them on historical choices and their possible ramifications. This knowledge reservoir aids them in making well-versed decisions when dealing with or navigating that software segment.

Beyond its directional utility, this chronicle also doubles up as an analytical instrument. Brigades can scrutinize bygone verdicts, deduce their resultant effects, and harness these discernments to cultivate more insightful decisions in ensuing ventures, sidestepping similar oversights or makeshift solutions.

Promote a Culture of Collective Ownership

The essence of collective ownership is that every participant in the development squad not only has the permission but also the duty to refine and enhance any section of the codebase. This approach is a shift from conventional structures where a designated person or subgroup had exclusive rights over a particular module or element.

When the entire squad feels a sense of ownership, there's a natural motivation to uphold superior code standards since everyone shares the responsibility. This unified accountability ensures that issues like bugs, code anomalies, or potential refinements are addressed in a timely manner, rather than awaiting a particular "custodian" to handle them.

Collective ownership cultivates an environment of teamwork. Coders are more motivated to solicit and offer insights, culminating in comprehensive dialogues and optimal choices.

Given that each individual has a vested interest in the code, challenges like bugs or technical debt are perceived as communal concerns. This perspective prompts a hands-on methodology in problem-solving, as opposed to deferring responsibility.

Educate Stakeholders

Often, stakeholders, especially those external to the coding brigade, prioritize tangible outcomes like functionalities or end-products. They might perceive efforts channeled towards mitigating technical debt as a hindrance or an unfruitful activity.

By acquainting stakeholders with the intricacies and ramifications of technical debt, coders can instill a collective appreciation of the software crafting journey. This encompasses delineating how unchecked technical debt might culminate in decelerated functionality creation, augmented bug incidence, and potential software performance degradation.

It's crucial to underscore that tackling technical debt isn't merely a task but a commitment to the long-term vitality of the software. While the immediate payoffs might not be glaringly evident, it predicates streamlined, hassle-free, and productive developmental cycles in subsequent phases.

Implement Automated Testing

Automated testing signifies the use of scripts or specialized tools to evaluate software autonomously, negating the need for manual perusal of each functionality. These evaluations span from unit tests, assessing isolated software segments, to comprehensive or holistic tests examining the entire software framework.

Concurrently with a developer's modification or feature inclusion, automated tests are activated. This mechanism bestows immediate insights on the implications of the new code, be it disrupting established functionalities or ushering in novel issues.

Automated evaluations guarantee consistent scrutiny of the software, ensuring each segment faces identical stringent checks every iteration. This regularity curtails human discrepancies and certifies that even seldom-accessed functionalities persistently undergo validation checks.

Courtesy of automated testing, coders gain the liberty to modify or restructure, fortified by the assurance of immediate alerts in case of anomalies. This flexibility results in accelerated developmental loops, bolder restructuring endeavors, and a fortified and robust code structure.

Chapter Eight: Through Challenges

When diving into the realm of Agile, there are certain pitfalls and misconceptions that many stumble upon, leading them away from the true essence of this methodology.

Misinterpreting Agile as a Silver Bullet: Many organizations fall into the trap of viewing Agile as an instant remedy for all their operational problems. It's as if some believe that by merely declaring themselves 'Agile', they'll automatically overcome any inefficiencies and roadblocks they face. This couldn't be further from the truth. Agile, at its core, is a set of practices and values designed to improve workflow and communication. ATo truly leverage its benefits, businesses must not only adopt its practices but also its ethos. Commitment is key, and stakeholders must brace for the reality that even within Agile, challenges will persist. It's about navigating these challenges more effectively, not erasing them.

Believing 'Agile' Means 'No Planning': There's a significant misconception that Agile implies a lack of planning or strategy. This misinterpretation can be costly. In truth, Agile prioritizes continuous and adaptive planning over rigid, long-term roadmaps. It's about responding to changes and adapting as required without being tied down to an inflexible plan. Organizations that misinterpret Agile's adaptive nature as an invitation to bypass planning altogether often find themselves in chaotic scenarios, where projects drift aimlessly and outcomes become unpredictable.

Overemphasis on Tools Over Principles: The market is replete with tools and platforms claiming to aid in Agile adoption. While many of these are useful, they are supplementary to the core principles of Agile. It's akin to using a sophisticated software suite without understanding its fundamental purpose or utility. When organizations prioritize tools above the underlying Agile tenets, they risk losing the essence of Agile. Remember, tools are meant to support and streamline the Agile process, not become a crutch or substitute for the genuine practices and values.

Ignoring Technical Excellence: There's a precarious balance to strike in Agile between speed and quality. While Agile does emphasize rapid iterations and quick deliveries, this should never be at the cost of product quality. Rushing a product or feature out the door without ensuring it meets the requisite quality standards can lead to multiple issues down the line, including technical debt – a term used to describe the future cost of correcting earlier shortcuts. Maintaining technical excellence ensures that while you're nimble, you're not cutting corners that might haunt you later.

Rigid Adherence to a Single Methodology: It's common to find proponents so enamored with a particular Agile methodology, be it Scrum, Kanban, or others, that they treat it as an unassailable scripture. This level of rigidity can be counterproductive. Imagine trying to fit a square peg into every hole, regardless of its shape; the results wouldn't be optimal. Different projects, teams, and organizational cultures may require different Agile flavors or even a combination of several. Staunchly sticking to the tenets of one methodology, without considering its applicability to a given context, can thwart the inherent flexibility that Agile promotes. It's essential to view these methodologies as guidelines, not immutable laws, and be open to adjusting them as the situation demands.

Neglecting Team Feedback: One of Agile's cornerstones is iterative feedback. The teams, being at the forefront of operations, often possess a treasure trove of insights that can sharpen processes, mitigate challenges, and capitalize on opportunities. Turning a deaf ear to this feedback is akin to navigating a ship while ignoring the crew's observations about looming icebergs or potential shortcuts. For Agile to truly flourish, there needs to be a culture where feedback is actively sought, genuinely valued, and promptly acted upon.

Isolating Agile Teams from the Rest of the Organization: Think of an organization as an intricate watch mechanism. If one cog (in this case, the Agile team) operates at a different rhythm from the others, the entire mechanism might malfunction. When Agile teams function in silos, detached from the broader organizational ecosystem, it can lead to misalignments. The rest of the organization, still anchored in traditional methodologies, might not interface smoothly with the Agile team. This disconnect can birth bottlenecks, miscommunication, and inefficient workflows. Ensuring that the Agile mindset permeates the entire organization, or at least establishing bridge mechanisms for smooth interfacing, is crucial.

Inadequate Communication: The spirit of Agile is built on the pillars of collaboration and communication. It's ironic, then, that some Agile teams grapple with communication breakdowns. Such lapses can result from myriad factors: lack of structured communication channels, infrequent check-ins, or even personal dynamics. Regardless of the cause, the effects can be detrimental. It's like trying to compose a symphony when the orchestra members aren't in tune with each other. Instituting regular touchpoints, ensuring clear documentation, and fostering an environment where open dialogue is encouraged are essential to sidestep this pitfall.

Fearing Change: Embracing change is woven into the fabric of Agile. It's about being malleable, quickly pivoting when required, and staying in step with evolving requirements or market dynamics. Teams that shudder at the prospect of change, often due to an attachment to a pre-decided path or feature set, risk becoming obsolete. Imagine charting a route based on yesterday's weather forecast and refusing to alter it despite today's storm warnings. Such an approach can lead to missed opportunities or, worse, detrimental outcomes. An Agile team's true strength lies in its ability to adapt and recalibrate in the face of change.

The Role of Feedback in Responding to Change

We're living in an era where change is the only constant. Industries that once seemed invincible are being reshaped by the tidal waves of technological innovations. From the far-reaching impacts of AI and blockchain to the swift market shifts triggered by global events, the landscape is perpetually evolving. Moreover, customer needs are not what they were even a decade ago; they change with every new trend, technological leap, or global circumstance. In such turbulent waters, navigating with an old map and refusing to adjust one's sails can lead an organization astray. Traditional models that depend on long-term plans crafted well in advance often find themselves grappling with irrelevance. Herein lies the genius of Agile. It doesn't advocate for throwing planning out of the window, but rather, it encourages flexibility and responsiveness. It's about drafting a plan but being prepared to redraft, adapt, and evolve as the tides change. In essence, Agile recognizes that while planning is crucial, the ability to respond to the ever-changing dynamics of our modern world is paramount.

Picture a ship trying to find its way amidst a stormy sea. The turbulent waters and howling winds make the path uncertain, even treacherous. In such a scenario, a lighthouse provides the much-needed direction, ensuring the ship doesn't veer off course or crash into unseen obstacles. Similarly, in the unpredictable world of product or service development, feedback acts as that lighthouse. Amidst the flux of shifting requirements, technological innovations, and market dynamics, feedback illuminates the path. It ensures Agile teams don't just drift aimlessly but instead navigate with purpose, continuously steering their course towards the ultimate goal: delivering unmatched value in sync with real-world needs.

Iterative Learning Through Feedback: Traditional development models can be likened to an artist unveiling a masterpiece after months of work, only to realize it's not what the audience wanted. The artist then faces the arduous task of making changes, which could be both time-consuming and costly. Agile adopts a diametrically opposite approach. Instead of waiting for the grand reveal, Agile believes in periodic showcases. Feedback is woven into every phase, be it the daily discussions, reviews after sprints, or deep-dive retrospectives. This way, the product or service is always in alignment, evolving in tandem with insights gathered at regular intervals. It's about ensuring that every step taken is in sync with market demands and stakeholder expectations.

Customer-Centric Development: The voice of the customer isn't a distant echo in the Agile realm; it's a chorus that resonates throughout the development cycle. Rather than assuming what the customer might want, Agile teams bring them into the fold. Regular increments of the product are showcased, and the feedback gathered isn't just noted down — it's integrated into the developmental DNA. This iterative approach ensures the end result isn't just a reflection of the customer's needs but often surpasses them, addressing nuances that might not have been explicitly voiced but were implicitly desired.

Constructive Internal Dynamics: While the product or service being developed is paramount, the machinery behind it — the team — is equally vital. Agile places significant emphasis on introspection. It's not just about "What can we do better for the customer?" but also "How can we work better together?" Retrospectives are not mere feedback sessions; they're constructive discussions aimed at honing team dynamics, refining processes, and ensuring that the journey is as impactful as the destination. It's about fostering a culture where continuous improvement isn't just encouraged but is ingrained.

Facilitating Proactive Risk Management: In the world of development, surprises are rarely pleasant. Left unchecked, minor hiccups can snowball into major roadblocks. With its pulse on feedback, Agile acts as a sophisticated radar system, detecting potential challenges well before they escalate. Whether it's a misalignment in expectations, a technical bottleneck, or an unforeseen market shift, the consistent feedback loop ensures that Agile teams are always a step ahead. It's not about scrambling for solutions when a crisis hits, but about preemptively strategizing, ensuring smooth sailing even when the waters get rough.

Feedback serves a dual purpose. On one hand, it's the compass that points out areas of improvement, potential pitfalls, and opportunities. But on the other, it's a call to action. Simply amassing feedback is like hoarding treasure without ever utilizing its value. The real merit of feedback lies in the tangible changes it inspires. It's not just about listening but also about understanding, internalizing, and then acting. Whether it's a design tweak, a recalibrated feature set, a methodological shift, or even a shuffle in team roles – acting on feedback is the bridge between identifying a gap and effectively bridging it. An organization that truly embodies the Agile spirit doesn't just welcome feedback; it treats it as a catalyst for transformation, ensuring that insights translate into meaningful actions.

Conflict Resolution and Effective Communication

Within the dynamic structure of Agile, team collaboration is of paramount importance. However, as with any group of individuals working closely together, disagreements are bound to emerge. These could stem from a multitude of reasons, be it clashing views regarding task priorities, variances in personal work habits, or even innocent misinterpretations. While these types of disagreements are commonplace in many team environments, their prominence is accentuated in Agile due to its unique iterative approach. This method, which demands consistent alignment among members, can inadvertently shine a spotlight on even minor misalignments, making conflict resolution crucial.

The Agile Manifesto, a seminal text in modern project management, extols the virtues of "individuals and interactions" over tools and processes. This, at its heart, is an appeal to the sanctity of human connections and interactions. Within this paradigm, the principle of openness becomes pivotal. To fully harness the power of Agile, there is an inherent need to cultivate an environment where team members feel empowered to voice even the minutest of concerns, or express dissenting opinions, without any looming trepidation of backlash. Such an atmosphere, imbued with trust, can preemptively address many conflicts before they escalate.

Amidst the hustle of recurrent stand-ups, sprint plannings, and reviews, the essence of conversations can often get lost in the cacophony. Instead of genuine dialogues, there's a risk of conversations becoming mere exchanges of rehearsed lines. This is where the subtle art of active listening steps in. It isn't merely about catching words; it's about grasping the underlying sentiments, questions, and concerns. When team members immerse themselves in the act of listening – absorbing and reflecting upon every word shared – they pave the way for deeper mutual respect and comprehension. This, in turn, becomes instrumental in dismantling conflicts at their roots, which more often than not are rooted in miscommunications.

Emotions are an intrinsic part of human nature. However, when discussions spiral into emotional territories, they can often veer off course, losing their constructive edge. Agile, with its intrinsic emphasis on results and deliverables, encourages its practitioners to steer discussions with a laser-focus on objectives. By centering debates around palpable elements - such as user stories, sprint goals, or product backlogs - teams can ensure that conversations remain tethered to productivity. This objective anchoring not only curtails the possibility of discussions becoming mired in emotional quagmires but also ensures a solution-oriented approach.

Agile methodology, provide teams with a neutral arena where every member can lay bare their thoughts, concerns, and suggestions. The structured nature of these sessions facilitates a climate where each voice is heard without the interruption of the daily hustle. Within this serene space, issues that could otherwise evolve into contentious debates are addressed, dissected, and solved in a collaborative spirit. This format not only ensures that potential conflicts are handled proactively but also reinforces the team's commitment to growth and learning.

The Alchemy of Constructive Feedback: In the Agile world, feedback is not just a mere mechanism for improvement; it's the pulse that keeps the methodology alive and thriving. But the magic lies not just in providing feedback, but in its artful delivery. By spotlighting the commendable aspects first, sandwiching actionable areas of enhancement, and abstaining from sweeping negative statements, feedback morphs into a tool for empowerment. It paves the way for open-minded reception, making sessions not just palatable but deeply insightful and free from the undertones of conflict.

In the dynamics of team interactions, occasionally, the maze becomes too intricate for members to navigate alone. When conflicts seem entrenched and resolution appears elusive, external intervention becomes more than a luxury—it's a necessity. This is the juncture where seasoned roles, like the Scrum Master or Agile Coach, come to the forefront. Armed with a bird's-eye view, they possess the unique ability to distil conflicts, ensuring every perspective is given its due consideration. Their impartial stance makes them the perfect mediators, guiding the ship through stormy waters towards a consensus that reflects the team's collective wisdom.

Strip away the processes, the methodologies, and the jargons, and at the heart of Agile lies the timeless principle of human interaction. Effective communication becomes the linchpin holding together the diverse tapestry of team dynamics. It's more than a mere exchange of words; it's an intricate dance of expressing and understanding, of speaking and listening. By cultivating a milieu of open-hearted dialogue, enveloped in empathy and mutual respect, Agile teams have the power to metamorphose conflicts. These once perceived impediments can be re-envisioned as stepping stones—leading to enhanced understanding, profound growth, and a collaborative spirit that resonates deeper than ever.

Overcoming Resistance to Change

Change, by its very nature, elicits a myriad of reactions from those it impacts. From the apprehensive reticence of some to the excited anticipation of others, its presence is rarely, if ever, unanimously welcomed. Within the world of Agile and project management, where change is not only expected but celebrated, resistance to it can be a significant roadblock. However, with the right strategies, this roadblock can be transformed into a stepping stone toward successful Agile implementation.

At the heart of human behavior is the desire for predictability and security. This is deeply rooted in our evolutionary past, where stability often meant safety from environmental threats. As a result, established routines and familiar workflows in the modern workplace offer comfort. Transitioning to new methods, especially significant shifts like adopting Agile practices, disrupts this familiarity. The result is a multifaceted emotional response, including anxiety stemming from the unknown, concerns over one's ability to adapt and excel in the new structure, and the unsettling feeling that comes with losing one's grip on previously mastered tasks.

Often, resistance is a byproduct of ambiguity. When teams don't fully grasp the rationale behind changes, skepticism grows.To alleviate this, it's essential to offer clear explanations about the decision to move to Agile – detailing not just the processes but also the strategic benefits. The objective is to paint a holistic picture: how will Agile benefit the organization, the individual teams, and the products or services being developed? By providing transparent reasons for the transition, you can address doubts and fears head-on.

A full-throttle shift to Agile can lead to information and process overload, making team members feel as though they've been thrown into the deep end. A more measured approach involves initiating Agile practices within a select group, perhaps a pilot team or a specific project. This allows for real-time feedback and fine-tuning of the process. As other teams witness the successes and challenges of the pilot group, they are better prepared for their transition. This also ensures that when Agile is rolled out on a larger scale, there's already a blueprint in place, refined by earlier experiences.

One of the significant barriers to accepting change is the fear of falling short, the worry that one might not have the skills to succeed in the new environment. To counter this, it's paramount to offer robust training programs. This not only equips team members with necessary Agile-specific skills but also rebuilds their confidence. Continuous learning opportunities, be they workshops, seminars, or peer-led sessions, ensure that every team member feels supported and competent in the evolving workspace.

At the heart of many successful organizational changes is a shared sense of ownership. When individuals feel that they've had a say in a decision, they naturally gravitate towards ensuring its success. When transitioning to Agile, it's beneficial to consult team members about the specific methodologies, tools, or practices being considered. This could be achieved through brainstorming sessions, surveys, or group discussions. When individuals see that their opinions are valued and incorporated, they are more likely to embrace the change and become its champions.

Celebrate early wins! Humans are inherently driven by results. When individuals can associate efforts with outcomes, they're more likely to appreciate and support the processes that led to those results. As teams begin to implement Agile practices, it's crucial to identify and spotlight positive outcomes, however minor they might seem. This could involve public recognition, sharing success stories in team meetings, or even small rewards. Such celebrations reinforce the effectiveness of Agile and provide motivation for its continued use.

Change, no matter how promising, can be daunting. Individuals might grapple with a myriad of emotions, from excitement to apprehension. Addressing these emotions requires a leadership approach rooted in empathy. This means setting up channels where team members can voice their anxieties, whether through individual check-ins, group discussions, or designated feedback sessions. For those finding the shift particularly challenging, offering additional support through coaching or mentoring can be invaluable.

Chapter Nine: Scaling Agile

Today organizations need frameworks that accommodate rapid change while maintaining efficiency, especially as they grow. While Agile methodologies like Scrum and Kanban are excellent for individual teams, larger enterprises often grapple with scaling these principles across multiple departments or even global locations. To address these challenges, several frameworks and models have emerged, aiming to imbue the Agile philosophy at an enterprise level. This chapter will provide an overview of three prominent ones: the Scaled Agile Framework (SAFe), Large-Scale Scrum (LeSS), and the Spotify Model.

Scaled Agile Framework (SAFe)

The Scaled Agile Framework, popularly known as SAFe, has emerged as a principal solution for large enterprises aiming to implement Agile practices beyond just a few teams. As organizations grow, so do their complexities, and SAFe seeks to address these intricacies. Rather than being a one-size-fits-all model, SAFe offers a structured yet adaptable approach, blending in aspects from multiple Agile methodologies along with lean product development.

SAFe categorizes its approach based on organizational hierarchy, ensuring that every level of the organization, from individual teams to the higher echelons of leadership, has clear Agile directives.

Team Level: At the ground level, teams operate much like traditional Agile teams, working in iterations and focusing on delivering increments of value.

Program Level: This involves multiple teams working together on larger initiatives, often coordinated through what SAFe refers to as an "Agile Release Train (ART)".

Large Solution Level: Ideal for vast enterprises, this level coordinates multiple ARTs to build significant, complex solutions.

Portfolio Level: At the top tier, the focus is on aligning the Agile initiatives with the overarching business strategy, ensuring that projects align with broader organizational goals.

What sets SAFe apart are the specific roles introduced to bridge the often-seen gap between development teams and the broader business.

Release Train Engineer (RTE): Think of them as the chief Scrum Masters for an Agile Release Train, ensuring that the train stays on track and meets its objectives.

System Architect: While individual teams might have architects, the System Architect looks at the broader picture, ensuring that all teams' efforts align into a coherent whole.

Beyond roles, SAFe emphasizes collaboration across all departments, ensuring that everyone from developers to stakeholders is on the same page.

Organizations transitioning to SAFe often report significant operational improvements.

Speed: With a clear framework in place, products and features often reach the market faster.

Productivity Boost: Clearer roles and alignment mean fewer roadblocks and more streamlined operations.

Quality Uptick: A coordinated approach reduces overlaps and redundancies, leading to a better end product.

Employee Satisfaction: With clearer guidelines and a sense of purpose, teams often report higher levels of engagement and job satisfaction.

Large-Scale Scrum (LeSS)

When organizations wish to extend the simplicity and effectiveness of Scrum beyond a single team, they often look towards Large-Scale Scrum (LeSS). The genius behind LeSS lies in its resistance to complicating the Scrum framework. Instead of inventing new roles or layers of management, LeSS suggests simply using the Scrum framework across multiple teams, effectively treating several teams as one large Scrum team.

The core philosophy of LeSS is not to reinvent the wheel but to keep the process lean and straightforward. By adhering to Scrum's foundational principles, even at scale, LeSS ensures that teams don't stray away from the tenets of transparency, empiricism, and continuous evolution. This approach ensures that even as teams grow and projects become complex, the process remains agile and uncomplicated.

With LeSS, everything that's familiar to a Scrum practitioner remains intact—sprint planning, daily stand-ups, sprint reviews, and retrospectives. But the scale introduces nuances. For instance:

Single Product Backlog: Multiple teams work from a single, unified product backlog, ensuring that everyone's focus remains on overarching product goals and not just isolated team objectives.

Coordination Events: While the individual teams conduct their daily stand-ups and reviews, LeSS introduces the "Overall Retrospective". This event is a gathering of representatives from all teams to discuss cross-team challenges and opportunities for overall improvement.

Here are the main advantages of LeSS:

Reduced Overhead: By not introducing a plethora of new roles or artifacts, LeSS keeps things streamlined, reducing the chances of overhead and bureaucracy.

Clearer Communication: With a unified product backlog and regular cross-team retrospectives, teams find it easier to stay aligned and avoid communication silos.

Customer-Centric Delivery: LeSS keeps the focus on delivering consistent value to the end customer, ensuring that large-scale operations don't compromise product quality or relevance.

Spotify Model

At a time when many organizations were grappling with scaling Agile, Spotify took inspiration from Agile principles but charted its own path. Their approach, while bearing the hallmarks of agility, was tailored to fit the company's distinct needs and culture. The result wasn't a rigid framework but a fluid model that emphasized team dynamics and organizational alignment, while also fostering a sense of ownership and innovation.

The Building Blocks: Squads, Chapters, Guilds, and Tribes

Imagine a small team, cross-functional and self-organizing, with a clear mission. This is a Squad. Each Squad owns a particular feature or a component of the product and works somewhat autonomously to achieve its goals.

Chapters: These can be visualized as horizontal layers cutting across Squads. For example, all backend developers from different Squads might form a Chapter, focusing on shared techniques, challenges, and competency growth.

Guilds: Guilds are more informal, wider networks that anyone in the organization can join based on interest. They're platforms for sharing knowledge, tools, and practices about specific topics.

Tribes: As the name suggests, Tribes are larger organizational entities. They are essentially a cluster of Squads, usually working in related areas or domains. Tribes ensure that while Squads work autonomously, there's still a sense of broader alignment and synergy.

Spotify's approach is a delicate balance between granting teams the freedom to decide their working methods while ensuring they're aligned with the broader organizational vision. It's a belief that teams, when given autonomy, can produce their best work. However, this autonomy isn't absolute. While the Squads might dictate their day-to-day operations (the 'how'), overarching goals and priorities (the 'what') are driven by the broader organizational strategy.

Advantages of the Spotify Model:

Innovation Thrives: By giving teams autonomy, the model creates an environment where new ideas and methods can be tested and adopted without undue bureaucratic hindrance.

Agility at Scale: Even as the organization grows, the modular nature of Squads and Tribes ensures agility isn't compromised.

Knowledge Flows: Through Chapters and Guilds, there's a continuous exchange of knowledge, ensuring that expertise isn't siloed and best practices permeate the organization.

Adaptability: The model's inherent flexibility means it can be adapted and tweaked based on specific organizational needs, making it relevant for a range of industries beyond just Spotify.

Coordinating Multiple Agile Teams

As Agile methodologies gain traction, many organizations find themselves at a crossroads where they're no longer coordinating the activities of just one Agile team, but multiple ones. The expansion from a single Agile team to several can be both an exciting opportunity and a daunting challenge. This metamorphosis presents its own set of complexities, but with the right strategies, the dance of multiple Agile teams can be as harmonious as a well-conducted orchestra.

While a single Agile team functions like a close-knit unit—self-organizing, communicating seamlessly, and delivering iteratively—multiple teams introduce interdependencies, overlapping responsibilities, and potential bottlenecks. The challenge lies not just in scaling up but in ensuring that the core principles of Agile are not diluted in the process.

Shared Vision and Goals: In any project, especially those that span multiple teams, a clear direction is paramount. This isn't just about understanding the end product but having clarity on the value it brings, the problem it solves, and its significance in the broader organizational strategy. Without a shared vision, teams can drift into isolated pockets, building features that might conflict or duplicate efforts. A unified understanding ensures every team member, irrespective of their role, knows the 'why' behind their 'what'. This often starts at the leadership or product owner level. Workshops, visual roadmaps, or even storytelling sessions can be effective ways to disseminate the vision across all teams.

Regular Cross-Team Meetings: Beyond the daily focus of individual team stand-ups, cross-team meetings, often termed "Scrum of Scrums", play a crucial role in larger projects. These meetings provide a platform to discuss interdependencies, synchronize efforts, and ensure that teams aren't working at cross-purposes. They act as early warning systems for potential blockers or misalignments. Typically, representatives from each team attend, discussing the work completed, the plan ahead, and any impediments faced. Depending on the project's complexity, these can be held daily or a few times a week.

Unified Backlog Management: While individual teams maintain their sprint backlogs, it's crucial to have a centralized product backlog. This master backlog ensures alignment on priorities and offers a holistic view of the product's progress and direction. It acts as a single reference point, ensuring teams are on the same page. A product owner or a chief product owner in larger settings usually maintains this. Regular backlog grooming sessions, with input from all teams, ensure it remains relevant and prioritized.

Integrated Demos: Beyond individual sprint reviews, integrated demonstrations offer a platform for teams to showcase their work collectively. Demos allow teams to see the bigger picture, understand how their contributions fit into the larger product mosaic, and ensure alignment in terms of functionality. Additionally, they foster a culture of collective ownership and pride. While the format can vary, it's vital to have a structured approach, ensuring each team gets a chance to showcase, and feedback loops are established. This not only fosters inter-team learning but also helps in spotting inconsistencies or integration challenges early on.

Dependency Management: In multi-team projects, dependencies are the ties that bind tasks across teams. They represent the interrelated nature of the work, where one team's output might be another's input. If these ties are overlooked or mismanaged, they can delay or derail the project, turning them into significant impediments. To better manage these dependencies, visualization becomes paramount. This is where tools such as Dependency Boards come in. Think of them as a visual map detailing how different teams or tasks are interlinked, offering a bird's-eye view of potential choke points or blockages. Another tool in the arsenal is DAGs (Directed Acyclic Graphs). As the name suggests, these graphs highlight dependencies in a directed manner, ensuring that there are no circular dependencies, making the project flow predictable.

Consistent Practices and Tools: If one team uses 'story points' for effort estimation while another uses 'hours,' it can make integrated planning cumbersome. Having consistent practices, tools, and terminologies doesn't mean stifling a team's unique approach. Instead, it's about establishing a common language for all teams, ensuring seamless integration. For example, while teams might have their internal tools, having a unified project management software or a shared definition of 'Done' can greatly streamline cross-team coordination.

Shared Metrics and Reporting: In a vast project landscape with multiple teams, it's easy to get lost in the details. While individual teams might be meeting their sprint goals, how does the project fare as a whole? This macro-level perspective becomes crucial for stakeholders, sponsors, and even team leads. A unified dashboard addresses this need. By pooling in data and key metrics from all teams, it provides a consolidated view of the project's health. Be it the cumulative velocity of all teams, the bug count, or the release readiness, a centralized dashboard offers a single source of truth. With this, stakeholders can make decisions not based on gut feelings but concrete data, ensuring that the project stays on course and resources are optimized.

Intra-team Feedback: Within teams, mechanisms like daily stand-ups, sprint reviews, and retrospectives serve as avenues for feedback. They ensure that the team learns from its experiences and implements these learnings in subsequent sprints.

Inter-team Feedback: When multiple teams work on interdependent tasks, it's essential to have feedback mechanisms that capture the bigger picture. Joint reviews, cross-team retrospectives, and shared backlog grooming sessions can serve this purpose. They ensure that as teams pivot based on feedback, they don't inadvertently step on each other's toes or move in divergent directions.

Measuring and Improving Performance at Scale

In the intricate ballet of Agile project management, especially when scaled, success isn't merely subjective. It's quantifiable. Metrics and measurements provide the compass by which Agile teams, no matter their size, can navigate the tumultuous waters of project execution, continuously recalibrating their course towards value delivery. Yet, as Agile scales, the complexity multiplies. How then do organizations measure and subsequently improve performance at this level?

Firstly, it's essential to grasp that simply multiplying the metrics of a single team does not necessarily translate when dozens, or even hundreds of teams, are in play. At scale, the dynamics change. Interdependencies can become bottlenecks; efficiencies might contradict across teams, and the nuances of performance take on a broader hue.

Key Performance Indicators (KPIs) at Scale

Velocity Across Teams: When discussing velocity across teams, it's important to recognize that velocity, by its original definition, quantifies the work a single team can achieve within a sprint. However, in a scenario with multiple teams, merely summing up individual velocities won't provide a comprehensive picture. By focusing on the aggregate velocity, which combines the capacities of all teams, we gain a clearer understanding of the entire project's pace. Furthermore, identifying disparities in velocities among different teams offers insights into potential challenges some teams might be facing, allowing leadership to intervene and provide necessary support or resources.

Enterprise-level Burn-Up and Burn-Down Charts: Moving on to enterprise-level burn-up and burn-down charts, these tools elevate the traditional agile metrics to a grander scale. Burn-down charts, conventionally used to illustrate remaining work in a sprint, and burn-up charts, showing the completed work, become exponentially valuable when we view them from an enterprise standpoint. They allow stakeholders to visualize the combined progress of all teams. Instead of focusing on singular team achievements, these charts provide a panoramic perspective of where the entire project stands in relation to its overarching goals.

Cycle Time and Lead Time: The differentiation between the two is subtle yet significant. Cycle time encompasses the duration from when a team starts working on a feature or story to its completion. In contrast, lead time commences the moment a new idea or feature is conceived and continues until its final delivery. At an enterprise level, understanding these metrics is paramount. It's not only about pinpointing the efficiency of the development process, represented by the cycle time, but also about assessing the overall efficiency from inception to delivery, encapsulated by the lead time. Longer lead times might indicate delays in the preliminary stages, be it in decision-making, approvals, or resource allocation.

Defect Density: Offers a lens through which the quality of delivery can be assessed. While speed and efficiency are crucial, they shouldn't come at the cost of quality. Defect density calculates the number of defects relative to the delivered functionality. This metric becomes especially pertinent when multiple teams are involved. It ensures that regardless of the team, the quality of delivery remains consistent. Monitoring defect density also aids in ensuring teams are learning from their mistakes and making efforts to elevate the quality of their work in subsequent sprints.

Time to Market: In today's business environment, time to market has grown increasingly significant, particularly for expansive enterprises contending in aggressive sectors. The essence of this metric lies in its ability to capture the entirety of a product's developmental journey, commencing from the mere spark of an idea and culminating in its final introduction to awaiting customers. Rapid time to market can be a clear indication of efficient processes and streamlined decision-making pathways, while prolonged durations might signal bottlenecks or inefficiencies.

Feedback Response Time: Feedback response time gains additional importance when an organization is spread across multiple teams or even geographical locations. In such environments, feedback isn't just about customer reviews or user insights; it's also about the internal feedback loop - the kind that flows between teams. The pace at which this feedback is processed and then embedded into the product or system becomes emblematic of the organization's agility and responsiveness. A delay could hint at communication breakdowns or a possible hesitation in decision-making, whereas promptness suggests a well-oiled machinery working in unison.

Escaped Defects: In the realm of software or product development, defects are an inevitable outcome, but escaped defects - those that elude internal detection and find their way to the end-user - deserve special attention. Such defects, when monitored, serve as a mirror reflecting the robustness of an organization's quality assurance mechanisms, especially when scaled up. If these defects are recurring or increasing, it may be time to revisit and potentially overhaul testing procedures and quality gates.

Team Engagement and Morale: Lastly, as with any endeavor, the human element remains paramount. In large-scale operations, maintaining a pulse on team engagement and morale becomes less of a luxury and more of a necessity. It's not just about productivity; it's about human well-being, satisfaction, and professional growth. Instruments like surveys can offer quantitative insights, while tools like the Niko-Niko Calendar—a visual tracker of team emotions—can shed light on the more qualitative, often nuanced facets of team sentiment. Ensuring that team members not only contribute effectively but also find joy and purpose in their roles is foundational to sustained success.

Strategies for Improving Performance at Scale

Centralized Visibility: In an age where data-driven decisions reign supreme, centralized visibility becomes the linchpin for enterprise success. When working with Agile tools at an organizational level, a central dashboard can serve as a beacon, shedding light on diverse metrics. This unifying perspective, more than just a visual representation, is instrumental in unveiling underlying patterns and disparities, and pinpointing areas ripe for enhancement. Such a consolidated viewpoint ensures that stakeholders aren't flying blind; instead, they are equipped with insights that empower them to steer their ship confidently through both calm and stormy waters.

Training and Upskilling: Beyond the world of dashboards and metrics, the prowess of an organization invariably hinges on its people. In this light, training and upskilling emerge as non-negotiable imperatives. By pouring resources into regular training interventions, organizations are essentially future-proofing themselves. They ensure that every team, regardless of where they stand on the experience spectrum, is in sync with industry best practices. Such a concerted effort in nurturing talent does more than just elevate skill sets; it fosters a culture of continuous learning and adaptation.

Standardization vs. Autonomy: Navigating between standardization and autonomy is no small feat. On one hand, setting certain benchmarks or standards acts as a cohesive force, binding different units of an organization with a shared language and approach. Such standards simplify coordination, minimize misunderstandings, and pave the way for a harmonized rhythm of work. On the flip side, the beauty of Agile lies in its inherent flexibility. Recognizing this, it's pivotal for organizations to grant their teams sufficient breathing space — the autonomy to mold, adapt, and innovate within the broader framework. By striking this delicate balance, businesses not only harness the efficiencies of a standardized approach but also ignite the creative sparks that often lead to groundbreaking innovations.

Review and Adaptation: Today, organizations that don't take the time to stop, review, and adapt risk being left behind. One way to ensure that processes remain efficient and relevant is to hold quarterly or bi-annual reviews at the enterprise level. This isn't just about taking a retrospective glance but rather a forward-facing assessment that gauges the effectiveness of methodologies, tooling, and the overall direction. It's akin to servicing a car; regular check-ups ensure that all parts function in harmony and any potential hitches are addressed before they evolve into more significant challenges.

Encourage Cross-team Collaboration: Creating silos within an organization can be detrimental. However, when you foster an environment of cross-team collaboration, the results can be transformative. Just as iron sharpens iron, teams can refine their strategies, practices, and approaches by learning from their peers. This collaboration isn't merely about problem-solving but also an avenue for sharing triumphs, innovative solutions, and lessons from failures. Such a culture doesn't just streamline operations but also engenders a sense of community and mutual growth.

Proactive Risk Management: When dealing with projects at scale, risks become inevitable. But what differentiates successful organizations from the rest is how they approach these risks. Rather than adopting a reactive stance, waiting for challenges to manifest, a proactive approach to risk management can be a game-changer. By identifying potential pitfalls early on and crafting strategies to either avoid or mitigate them, organizations can deftly navigate the often-tumultuous waters of large-scale projects. It's the difference between weathering a storm with a sturdy ship and a clear map versus being caught unawares.

Stakeholder Engagement: Lastly, but by no means least, is the pivotal role of stakeholder engagement. From the corridors of top-tier management to the invaluable feedback of the end customer, ensuring all voices are heard is crucial. This isn't just about collecting feedback but actively engaging these stakeholders in the journey. Their insights, criticisms, and commendations set the direction, ensuring that the enterprise remains aligned with its broader goals and the evolving needs of its customer base. When stakeholders are not just spectators but active participants, it provides a holistic view that's invaluable for any organization.

Bonus Chapter: Agile in Non-Software Domains

The Agile movement, birthed in the realm of software development, has a reputation firmly rooted in iterative development, sprints, and user stories. Yet, at the core of Agile lies a set of principles and values that transcend code and computers. As industries evolve in the face of rapid technological and societal changes, the desire for more flexible, adaptable, and customer-centric approaches has led to the application of Agile principles in a multitude of fields outside of software. But how do these principles translate, and where have they found a foothold?

Agile in Marketing

In today's bustling digital landscape, the marketing realm has experienced unprecedented changes. Gone are the days when marketers would laboriously craft extensive campaigns, only to realize that by the time they were executed, consumer sentiments had shifted. Instead, there's a rising clamor for a nimble approach, one that can deftly pivot with the ever-evolving tastes and trends of the modern consumer. Enter Agile marketing, a beacon of adaptability in this era of rapid change.

Drawing inspiration from its software development roots, Agile marketing employs shorter cycles of planning and execution known as "sprints." These aren't just abbreviated timelines; they're incubators for innovation. Within each sprint, marketing teams test a multitude of ideas, throwing them into the crucible of the real marketplace, not just theoretical boardrooms. This approach yields a treasure trove of real-world data, which becomes the bedrock for refining subsequent strategies.

But what truly sets Agile marketing apart is its inherent synchronicity with the zeitgeist. By operating in these compressed cycles, campaigns resonate more deeply with current events, cultural shifts, and emerging preferences. It's akin to having one's finger constantly on the pulse of society, ensuring campaigns are not just timely but also topical. Moreover, this dynamic methodology ensures a judicious use of resources. Rather than pouring funds and energy into potentially outdated campaigns, real-time feedback guides marketing endeavors, leading to more targeted, effective, and financially sound decisions. In essence, Agile marketing isn't just a strategy; it's the art of dancing gracefully with change.

Agile and HR

Today, the sphere of Human Resources is experiencing a transformative overhaul. Gone are the days when HR was just a custodian of paperwork, policies, and payroll. With the advent of the modern workforce, characterized by its fluidity, hunger for growth, and an undeniable quest for a wholesome 'employee experience,' HR had to reinvent its strategies. This imperative gave birth to the concept of Agile HR, a symbiotic blend of HR's core principles with the nimbleness of Agile methodologies.

Instead of the once-a-year performance check-ins that often felt detached and retrospective, Agile HR champions the ethos of regular and meaningful feedback. This shift ensures that employee performance, aspirations, and areas of development are discussed in real-time, leading to timely interventions and, more importantly, a sense of being valued. But that's just one facet of it.

Recruitment, a cornerstone of HR, has also been touched by Agile's transformative spirit. Hiring processes are no longer linear or siloed. They've metamorphosed into dynamic strategies that change as per the organization's evolving needs, ensuring that the talent brought on board is not just right for today but also for tomorrow's challenges. And while recruitment remains a significant aspect, Agile HR recognizes that the real magic happens post-hiring. It's all about crafting a culture – an ambiance where employees don't just work but thrive.

The underpinnings of Agile HR are collaboration and adaptability. It's about breaking down the proverbial walls and fostering a space where cross-functional teams, continuous learning, and innovation are the norm. And at the heart of it all lies the principle of continuous improvement. In the Agile HR universe, resting on laurels isn't an option. Every process, every strategy is in a state of perpetual evolution, ensuring that the HR function is not just responsive but also proactive, readying the organization for both the challenges and opportunities of tomorrow.

Agile in Manufacturing

In manufacturing, the introduction of Agile methodologies has been nothing short of revolutionary. Historically, manufacturing was characterized by long, often inflexible production cycles. Every product had a rigid path from conceptualization to creation, with little room for deviation. However, with the evolution of market demands and technological advancements, there arose a pressing need for more adaptive strategies. This is where Agile, with its roots deeply influenced by Lean Manufacturing, began to make its presence felt.

The essence of Lean Manufacturing, with its focus on minimizing waste and maximizing efficiency, seamlessly blended with Agile's core tenets. Together, they championed the cause of not just producing more in less time but producing what genuinely resonates with the market pulse. This paradigm shift ushered in the era of iterative prototyping. Instead of dedicating extensive resources to produce a final product in one go, manufacturers started building preliminary versions or prototypes. These prototypes were then exposed to real-world users, stakeholders, and sometimes even to select market segments to gather firsthand feedback.

This feedback mechanism, inherent to the Agile approach, ensured two critical things. First, manufacturers could continually refine their designs based on actual market responses, ensuring that the final product wasn't just built to specifications, but to resonate with genuine consumer needs. Second, by adapting in real-time, resources—both material and human—were used more judiciously, minimizing the risks associated with large-scale production of an untested product.

But Agile's influence in manufacturing isn't just limited to the product design phase. Its collaborative spirit has reshaped the very ethos of the manufacturing floor. In this new world, silos have been dismantled. A designer isn't isolated from an engineer, nor is the engineer disconnected from the frontline worker. There's a harmonious, cross-functional collaboration where information and insights flow seamlessly. Everyone, regardless of their position or role, is aligned with the overarching goal: to produce not just efficiently, but also effectively, ensuring that every product that rolls off the line meets both quality standards and market expectations.

Cases of Success

Agile methodology's metamorphosis from a software-specific strategy to a ubiquitous approach for operational excellence is a testament to its adaptability and effectiveness. As businesses across the spectrum adopt Agile principles, their success stories offer invaluable insights. Here are some compelling cases that demonstrate the versatility of Agile in non-software areas.

The Automotive Giant: Tesla Motors

Tesla Motors stands as a testament to how innovative thinking, when melded with the right approach, can redefine an industry. At its core, Tesla may be a car manufacturer, but its approach to production diverges sharply from traditional automotive companies. The secret sauce to Tesla's success, beyond its emphasis on electric vehicles and sustainable energy, has been its incorporation of Agile methodologies, not just in the realm of software development but deeply ingrained in its manufacturing ethos.

The beauty of Agile lies in its capacity to iterate rapidly, to adapt based on feedback, and to always be in a state of evolution. Tesla, recognizing the transformative power of this methodology, has woven it into the fabric of its production process. When we look at how they develop their vehicles, the Agile influence is undeniable. Unlike traditional car manufacturers that may take years to refine and release new models or features, Tesla's approach is reminiscent of a tech startup. They roll out a prototype, gather feedback, refine, and iterate. This cycle of continuous improvement has allowed them to make bold strides in areas that many automotive giants tread cautiously, a prime example being their advancements in autonomous driving.

But Tesla's agility isn't confined to its vehicle design alone. A glance at their Gigafactory provides another layer of insight into their embrace of Agile principles. The Gigafactory is not just a marvel in terms of scale but also in adaptability. Production lines at the factory are not set in stone; they evolve based on real-time challenges, feedback from engineers on the floor, and the ever-changing demands of the electric vehicle market. This flexibility means that when a bottleneck appears or a component needs changing, the entire process can pivot swiftly, minimizing downtime and ensuring that production keeps pace with demand.

In a nutshell, Tesla's journey in the automotive industry, marked by its rapid innovation and adaptability, offers a clear blueprint of what's possible when the principles of Agile are applied beyond software, reshaping the very foundations of car manufacturing.

Retail Revolution: John Lewis & Partners

In the bustling retail of the UK, the name John Lewis & Partners carries with it a weight of tradition and a reputation for quality. Yet, even such stalwart institutions recognize the need for change when faced with the mercurial nature of modern commerce. At the heart of John Lewis's recent transformation is an unexpected ally: Agile methodology, typically hailed in the realms of software and tech but proving its worth in the tangible aisles of retail as well.

Historically, the supply chain in retail was a well-oiled machine, albeit one that ran on a fixed track. John Lewis, like many, followed this structured, linear model. Predict, procure, store, and sell — this was the set rhythm. However, the digital age, with its rapid shifts in consumer behavior and the unpredictable ebbs and flows of demand, posed challenges that this traditional model was ill-equipped to handle. Enter Agile.

The transition wasn't just about slapping on a set of new tools or practices but required a fundamental rethinking of operations. At the core of this shift was the formation of cross-functional teams. By bringing together diverse expertise — from procurement specialists to store managers to data analysts — these teams could tackle challenges holistically. No longer was decision-making confined to boardrooms or siloed departments. Instead, with an Agile mindset, solutions emerged from collaborative brainstorming, rapid prototyping, and constant iteration.

But how does one measure success or track progress in such a dynamic environment? Visual management tools became the answer for John Lewis. By visualizing workflows, tracking inventory in real-time, and mapping customer feedback directly onto their supply chain processes, the retail giant could spot bottlenecks, anticipate shortages, and adapt with a nimbleness previously thought impossible for an entity of its size.

The results of this Agile transformation spoke for themselves. Delivery times, once beholden to the whims of a sprawling supply chain, became more predictable and, in many cases, faster. The bane of all retailers — excess inventory, which represented tied-up capital and potential waste — was dramatically reduced. Most importantly, by being attuned to market trends in real-time and allowing feedback to guide their offerings, John Lewis ensured its products and services remained in lockstep with what the customer truly desired.

In essence, John Lewis & Partners' foray into Agile is a shining testament to the fact that even age-old institutions, with the right mindset and methodologies, can reinvent themselves to thrive in the modern marketplace.

Healthcare Transformation: Cerner Corporation

In the crossroads of healthcare and information technology lies Cerner Corporation, a company that has carved a niche for itself in the realm of health IT. At first glance, Cerner's core offering, software, might seem distant from the immediacy of hands-on medical care. Yet, as any healthcare professional would attest, the reliability and efficacy of health information technologies play an indomitable role in patient outcomes.

Traditionally, software development in the healthcare domain followed a cautious pace, a reflection of the critical nature of its application. Changes were deliberated extensively, and launches were buffered with significant lead times to account for the potential risks. But as the healthcare landscape grew more complex and dynamic, this sedate pace became a hindrance. Medical professionals, amidst emergencies and split-second decisions, required tools that could keep up, offering them the latest in diagnostics, patient history, and treatment recommendations.

Cerner recognized this palpable need for speed, accuracy, and adaptability. Their solution? Embracing the Agile methodology, a system that, until then, was primarily associated with the fast-paced world of tech startups and not the meticulous corridors of healthcare.

With Agile, Cerner didn't merely expedite its software development process. The approach ushered in a culture of continuous feedback and iteration. Each module or update, instead of being finalized in isolation, was tested, refined, and retested in real-world scenarios, ensuring its alignment with the immediate needs of healthcare providers. This shift was more than procedural; it was philosophical. Cerner began to see its software not as a static product but as a living entity, evolving in tandem with the ever-shifting world of medicine.

The benefits of this Agile transformation became evident swiftly. Healthcare professionals found that the tools at their disposal were not just modern but also anticipatory, often catering to needs they hadn't yet verbalized. In situations where seconds could spell the difference between life and death, having access to accurate, real-time information became a game-changer.

Cerner's journey with Agile is a testament to the fact that even in sectors where precision is paramount, adaptability and rapid evolution are not just possible but essential. By bridging the worlds of healthcare and Agile software development, Cerner reinforced the belief that with the right methodologies, technology can truly be a life-saving ally.

Final Word

As we turn the final page of this exploration into Agile, it's important to reflect upon the core truths that have been illuminated throughout this way. We live in an era marked by rapid change, where adaptability and responsiveness are not just advantageous but essential. In this context, Agile emerges not just as a methodology, but as a mindset that paves the way for organizations and individuals to thrive amidst uncertainty.

We've seen how Agile principles have been applied across a myriad of sectors, from its birthplace in software development to its innovative applications in marketing, HR, and manufacturing. This universality underscores a foundational truth: at the heart of Agile is the pursuit of delivering value, and this pursuit is relevant irrespective of the domain or discipline.

It's worth emphasizing that while tools, techniques, and frameworks play a pivotal role, the true essence of Agile lies in its people-centric approach. It's about teams that are empowered and aligned with a shared vision. It's about creating an environment where feedback is not just encouraged but celebrated, where failures are viewed as opportunities for growth, and where the customer's voice is central to decision-making.

For those who are just beginning their Agile journey, be prepared for challenges. Like any transformative approach, it requires effort, commitment, and sometimes a cultural shift. But as countless organizations and case studies have shown, the rewards—both tangible and intangible—are profound.

To those well-versed in Agile, let this book serve as a reminder of its foundational principles and as an inspiration to continually seek ways to refine and adapt your practices. Remember, the landscape of business and technology is in perpetual motion. Staying still equates to falling behind. The spirit of continuous improvement, a cornerstone of Agile, must be woven into the fabric of your organizational culture.

The world may be rife with complexities and challenges, but with an Agile mindset, we are better equipped to navigate them, delivering value and excellence every step of the way. Let's carry forward the lessons learned and embrace the future with confidence and agility.

www.ingramcontent.com/pod-product-compliance
Lightning Source LLC
Chambersburg PA
CBHW050451290526
45786CB00006B/2246